Dissertation Research

Dissertation Research

An Integrative Approach

Robert E. Levasseur, Ph.D.

MindFire Press
St. Augustine, Florida

ISBN–13: 978–0–9789930–3–0

Library of Congress Control Number: 2011914594

Published by MindFire Press— St. Augustine, Florida
(www.mindfirepress.com)

I dedicate this book to my wife, Donna Fox,
whose love, encouragement, and support
made my doctoral journey possible.

Contents

Preface

The dissertation is a daunting challenge. However, because the successful completion of the dissertation is necessary to move from ABD (All But the Dissertation) status to Ph.D. status (or the equivalent), there is no doubt that doctoral students are motivated to learn how to meet this challenge.

Despite the best efforts of universities to prepare them for this "final examination" of their doctoral studies, most doctoral students, regardless of how well they have done in their course work or on the major papers or exams that comprise the earlier part of their doctoral program, have very little idea when they reach the dissertation stage of (a) how to identify a suitable topic, or (b) how to design, conduct, and report the findings of an acceptable dissertation research project based on that topic.

This is primarily because the dissertation is like no other deliverable they have worked on before. As a result, students must learn both what it is as well as how to get it done. Contributing to the challenge is the fact that the resources at their disposal (i.e., rubrics, process diagrams, and the like provided by their university, and available reference books on the dissertation review process) tend either to (a) provide general descriptions of what they must produce (i.e., deliverables) at each stage of the dissertation review process without explaining how to produce them, or (b) provide detailed information on certain aspects of the process (such as how to write a literature review, or how to choose the right statistical method) without dealing with the dissertation research process holistically.

What most doctoral students need, and what my mentees have found most useful, is a more integrated, systemic, problem-solving approach based on the essential steps in the research process. Hence, the purpose of this book is to try to demystify dissertation research by (a) describing a simple, systemic, integrative approach to doctoral research, (b) providing examples of how to apply it effectively in qualitative, quantitative, and mixed methods research studies to harness personal passion and scholarly pursuit, and (c) providing students with the tools they need to apply the integrated process to their own dissertation research.

Studying this integrated process and learning how to apply it to concrete research topics will enable students to identify a researchable topic for their unique dissertation study that is rooted in their passion and grounded in the literature of their field, and that they, as scholars in pursuit of the highest educational degree, can fashion into a doable, high quality dissertation research project.

Part I

Dissertation Research

Chapter 1

What is a Dissertation?

Which of the following best describes a dissertation?

A. A requirement for the doctoral degree.

B. The deliverable of the capstone project of a doctoral program of study.

C. The equivalent of the "final examination" for a doctoral student.

D. The demonstration of a doctoral student's ability to design, conduct, and report the findings of a research project.

E. An attempt to advance the boundaries of knowledge in a given field under the guidance of a committee of fellow scholars.

F. A scholarly report, generally consisting of five chapters that provide (a) an overview of a research project, (b) a review of relevant literature, (c) a detailed description of the research methods used, (d) an explanation of the results obtained, and (e) the conclusions drawn from these findings as well as recommendations for professional application and further study.

G. An exercise in complex problem solving and decision making.

H. All of the above.

[Note: The answer is on the next page.]

The correct answer is H.

Because of the inherent complexity of this major undertaking, it is essential to approach the dissertation in a systematic fashion. The problem is to figure out how to do it.

One solution, which is based on the techniques of complex problem solving and decision making used by engineers and others who encounter these types of problems frequently, is to use an iterative process that takes a systemic view of dissertation research and moves in a logical, step-by-step manner from an initial broad statement of a problem of interest to a final, detailed dissertation design that, when executed properly, results in the creation of new knowledge about the problem and its solution.

While each dissertation journey is unique and filled with its own special challenges, the odds of solving the problems presented by a dissertation research study and completing the journey successfully are dramatically higher if you follow a systematic process like the one described in the next chapter.

Chapter 2

Dissertation Research: A Systemic View

One of the characteristics of systems that we are all familiar with is the fact that the parts of a system are interconnected. As a result, a change in one part of the system affects the other parts of the system to varying degrees. In this chapter, we will examine the dissertation research process from this point of view.

The table below briefly describes the 10 steps in the dissertation research process.

Table 1. Dissertation Research Process

#	Step	Description
1	Problem	Define the broad problem and its significance.
2	Grounding Literature	Ground the study in the existing literature.
3	Purpose	Specify the research focus.
4	Research Questions	Describe the research questions (and hypotheses).
5	Research Method	Select the general approach.
6	Research Design	Describe the essential design elements of the study.
7	Proposal	Create the detailed research plan.
8	Research	Conduct the study.
9	Dissertation	Present the findings.
10	Publication	Publish the findings.

The first seven steps in the dissertation research process are planning steps. The first six taken together constitute the integrated research plan (IRP). The seventh or proposal step results in a detailed research plan based on the IRP. The eighth is an action step involving the implementation of the research design. The final two are the reporting steps, in which a doctoral student communicates in a dissertation, and later possibly in one or more academic publications, the research and its findings in a form suitable to the intended audience.

For the dissertation, this typically takes the form of a five-chapter scholarly report addressed to other scholars, such as the dissertation committee and university appointed reviewers. In some cases, it also includes the preparation of one or more articles suitable for publication in refereed journals.

[Note: The dissertation research process described above is the same one that academic researchers follow when conducting and reporting the findings of their research to other scholars, except that it includes the additional steps (#7 and #9 in Table 1) of writing and defending a proposal and dissertation.]

When viewed from a systemic perspective, the dissertation research process is:

- ✓ Sequential
- ✓ Iterative
- ✓ Coherent

The dissertation research process is *sequential* in the sense that each step depends upon (i.e., aligns with) the preceding steps. That is, the search for the grounding literature focuses on the broad problem area specified in the problem statement. The purpose statement derives from the findings of the literature search. The research questions derive from the purpose of the study. The research method follows directly from the research questions. The research design actualizes the research method. The proposal ties all of the preceding steps into a detailed research plan. The research study implements the research plan. And, finally, the dissertation and publication present the findings of the research study to other scholars inside and outside of the university.

As shown in Figure 1, the dissertation research process is also *iterative* (i.e., trial and error) in the sense that circumstances uncovered when working on a given process step may necessitate the revision of one or more preceding steps, which in turn may necessitate the revision of subsequent steps.

For example, a careful literature search might lead to the conclusion that other scholars had studied a problem extensively and that, therefore, the answers to that problem exist in the literature, necessitating a shift to another dissertation topic. Or, the discovery of a problem in the design phase, such as the unavailability of existing quantitative data for one or more essential variables in the study, might necessitate a switch to a new research method (e.g., from existing data analysis to survey research).

A more complicated hypothetical example might involve the discovery in the pilot phase of a survey design process that a qualitative, interview-based approach would yield more valid data than the initially planned quantitative survey. This would almost certainly necessitate changes to the research questions, which in turn would require changes in the research method and the research design.

1. Problem
2. Grounding Literature
3. Purpose
4. Research Questions
5. Research Method
6. Research Design
7. Proposal
8. Research
9. Dissertation
10. Publication

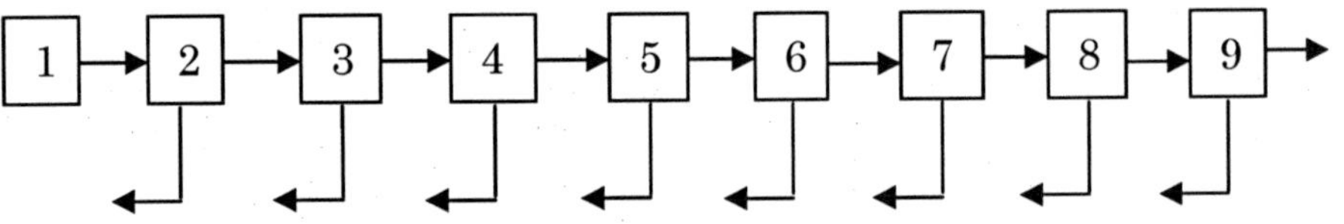

Figure 1. Systemic View of the Dissertation Research Process

Finally, the dissertation research process is *coherent* in the sense that when applied properly it results in a good "fit" among all of the elements of the process—the problem statement, grounding literature, purpose statement, research questions (and hypotheses), research method, research design, proposal, research, dissertation, and publication.

Now that you know something about the steps in the dissertation research process and its characteristics when viewed from a system perspective, we can move on to a more in-depth examination of each step without getting lost in the details. If you find this happening to you, simply return to this chapter, much as you might refer to a road map on a trip if you found yourself confused about which route to follow to arrive at your final destination.

Chapter 3

Dissertation Research: An Analytical View

In this chapter, we will examine each of the steps in the dissertation research process in detail, with an eye to developing an understanding of the function of each and its connection to other steps in the process. This will be an active process in which you participate by completing various exercises designed to enable you to focus in on a specific research design for your unique dissertation study.

1. Problem

We begin where you most likely are, by assuming that you have a passion for learning as much as you can about a "big idea," and for using that knowledge to obtain your doctorate and, eventually, change the world in some tangible, positive way.

For me, that big idea was to assess the impact of transforming leadership on follower performance and satisfaction. I could not understand why something that in my experience as a leader and change management consultant was so important and so effective was not more pervasive in society. By quantifying its often dramatic impact on productivity and morale, I hoped to make a stronger case for the use of transforming leadership in all organizations.

For some of my students, the big idea has been a topic like:

- ✓ Measuring how emotional intelligence and cultural intelligence affect leadership effectiveness in international settings

- ✓ Identifying strategies for enhancing the likelihood of successful mergers and acquisitions
- ✓ Examining the role of the Information Systems department in the success or failure of business process reengineering projects
- ✓ Assessing the effectiveness of school feeding programs in a major Canadian city and determining the reasons why they work or don't
- ✓ Quantifying the relationship between investments in quality and resulting product costs
- ✓ Assessing the relationship between spirituality and servant leadership among small business entrepreneurs
- ✓ Investigating how employees cope effectively with IT-driven change
- ✓ Quantifying the relationship between emotional intelligence and transformational leadership in project management

So, what are you passionate about? What important, socially significant problem do you want to study in depth and become a leading expert on as a result of your dissertation research?

It is important to stop reading now in order to take a few minutes to complete Exercise 1.1. This will enable you to capture the essence of your big ideas that meet the twin criteria of (a) being important problems to solve that (b) you are passionate about.

EXERCISE 1.1

Identifying Potential Research Topics

✓ Make a list of potential problems that meet these two criteria (i.e., they are important and you are passionate about them).

✓ Prioritize your list.

✓ Write a brief description (i.e., no more than a paragraph) of each problem based on your understanding of it at this time. [Note: This is an iterative process, so you can always come back and refine any of your descriptions later. But for now, you need to write an initial problem statement for each potential research topic.]

✓ Set aside your problem statements and continue reading.

While it should serve as a source of great energy and determination, having a big idea is the first step, not the last one, in your search for a dissertation topic. In fact, to paraphrase Mark Twain, the difference between having a doable, researchable dissertation topic and having a broadly defined problem (i.e., a big idea) that you want to study is like the difference between lightning and the lightning bug.

Once you have a problem statement that you are excited about, you then have to find out if anyone else in the research community is too. You do this by conducting an effective search of the literature related to your topic to find the grounding literature for your potential study.

2. Grounding Literature

The reason for conducting a literature search is to ground your proposed dissertation research in the literature of your field of interest. To understand why this is necessary, we need to examine the four basic ways that a big idea can translate into the domain of scholarly research. For the sake of discussion, let us refer to these four possibilities or cases as follows:

A. Old News

B. Out to Sea

C. A Hard Sell

D. An Easier Sell

We will assume for now that you know how to do an effective literature search using online databases, so that we can focus on the inherent differences among these four cases. [Note: See Appendix A for an explanation of the steps in the important process of performing a good online database search.]

Simply put, your goal in this second step of the dissertation research process is to search the literature (primarily peer-reviewed journals and dissertations) for prior research on your topic (i.e., your big idea). This search process, when it is successful, grounds your research in the literature.

A literature search will result in one of four generic outcomes listed above. We will examine each one in turn.

Case A: Old News

Based on your literature search, you discover that many studies exist on your topic. In fact, one or more of them provide definitive answers on the subject.

In 2002, when I did a literature search for my dissertation on the relationship between cooperative styles of leadership and more traditional, confrontational styles, I discovered a journal article (Johnson & Johnson, 1989) which reported that researchers had already conducted over 500 empirical primary studies on my topic, and over a decade earlier to boot. That was the end of my first big idea—to do a primary research study (i.e., original research) on that topic.

If you discover that your big idea is not new, and you persist in asking for permission to do yet another research project on it, you run the risk of having the faculty at your university ask the dreaded "Who cares?" question. If you cannot provide a solid rationale for how your dissertation study would enhance existing knowledge on the subject in response to this question (which might be difficult if not impossible to do under these circumstances), then the faculty will most likely not allow you to study that topic for your dissertation.

Case B: Out to Sea

Based on your literature search, you discover that there are no studies on your topic in the literature. Furthermore, there are not even any related studies on the topic.

If this happens, using the analogy that terra firma represents the domain of existing research literature, you are so far away from dry land that you once again run the real risk that the faculty will ask you, "Who cares?" As you are not likely to have a good answer to this question, you will probably not receive permission to proceed with your study of this topic.

Case C: A Hard Sell

Based on your literature search, you discover that there are several studies on topics that relate to your topic. However, none of them deals directly with your big idea. Hence, there is a definite gap in the literature that your study could fill.

This case, although researchable in the sense that it will make a contribution to the literature of the field, is sometimes difficult to sell because you must very carefully survey the existing literature before you can make a convincing argument that (a) there is a gap, and (b) your study will most likely fill it. The faculty will undoubtedly expect you to have done a very thorough search for articles, dissertations, and unpublished literature on the subject before giving you permission to proceed with your dissertation research.

Case D: An Easier Sell

Based on your literature search, you discover that there are one or more studies on your topic in the literature. However, none of them deals with the subject in quite the way that you intend to approach it. Perhaps one or more of these studies even calls, in its recommendations for further research, for a study of the type you hope to conduct.

This is the ideal situation that budding researchers hope to discover when they do a literature search. It is truly a Eureka! moment when you discover that such a study exists.

After months of trial and error spent trying to ground studies of many potential dissertation topics (I did not know about the database search process described in Appendix A at the time), when I finally found the article (DeGroot, Kiker, & Cross, 2000) that would serve as the basis for my dissertation work (by grounding it in the literature), I was ecstatic. To paraphrase Sir Isaac Newton, I had found the giants on whose shoulders I would attempt to stand.

Convincing faculty that your topic (i.e., big idea) is worth researching is much easier when you can point to a current (i.e., published in the past 5 years) peer-reviewed article or a dissertation that you intend to build upon in doing your dissertation research. For example, if an existing quantitative study on your topic discovered several interesting but unexplained findings based on an analysis of survey data, perhaps you might suggest a qualitative study based on face-to-face interviews that would examine these issues in more depth. Alternatively, if an existing qualitative study on your topic proposed an interesting and seemingly plausible theory, you might suggest a quantitative study that would test one or more hypotheses logically derived from that theory. Yet another approach might be to replicate the original study, but on a different population. As you can imagine, there are usually numerous possibilities for extending existing research studies.

In the case of my dissertation, I was able to extend the work of DeGroot, Kiker, and Cross (2000), among other ways, by incorporating 5 years worth of additional primary research studies on the topic, and by applying the latest meta-analytic techniques. Now it is time for you to complete Exercise 1.2 to try to ground your potential research topics.

EXERCISE 1.2

Grounding Your Ideas in the Literature

- ✓ Applying the method described in Appendix A to your highest priority potential research topic, search scholarly databases for peer-reviewed journal articles and dissertations on that topic that might serve to ground your dissertation research in the literature.
- ✓ Repeat this search process for each of your other high potential research topics.
- ✓ As a result of this process, if you downgrade or discard one or more of the topics on your original list of potential research topics in favor of one or more new topics uncovered by your search, then reprioritize your list and write a problem statement for each new topic.
- ✓ Set aside each problem statement and its associated grounding literature summary and continue reading.

3. Purpose

Once you have grounded your dissertation topic in the literature, you must describe exactly what you intend to study in your dissertation research project and how you intend to study it. You cannot describe the purpose of your research unless you have identified the place in the literature that your work will occupy. Your purpose statement must speak precisely to the gap in the research literature you intend to fill (Case C) or the boundary of knowledge that you intend to extend (Case D). Hence, stating that the purpose of your research is to eradicate world hunger or eliminate the scourge of AIDS, while laudable, would not as a purpose statement for your research project.

You must also identify in your statement of purpose whether your research will be a qualitative, quantitative, or mixed methods study; as well as the phenomenon you will study (if you are proposing a qualitative study), or the research variables and their interrelationships, such as the independent and dependent variables and any moderator or intervening variables (if you are proposing a quantitative study), or both (if you are proposing a mixed methods study).

For the sake of illustration, here is a portion of the justification for my dissertation (Levasseur, 2004, pp. 3–4), which dealt with a meta-analysis (i.e., aggregate analysis) of existing primary studies on my topic (i.e., the effect of transforming leadership on follower performance and satisfaction):

> Nevertheless, this body of literature has not been subjected to a meta-analysis since 1997 (DeGroot, Kiker, & Cross, 2000). Since then, new primary studies that attempted to measure the follower outcomes of transforming leadership, based both on experimental and correlational research designs, have been published . . . . Subjecting the results of these and earlier studies to the test of a new meta-analysis may provide the quantitative justification for a transforming leadership style over a traditional leadership style in much the same way that meta-analysis has provided support for the efficacy of new drugs or the benefits of new social programs . . . .

To summarize, the purpose statement for your study must identify how your dissertation research will extend the boundaries of existing knowledge based on the work that other researchers have already done in your field. To do this, you must first identify a broad professional problem area or issue that interests you and then ground your work by searching the literature of your field for existing studies on or related to that topic. Finally, you must describe the purpose of your unique dissertation research project in a way that links it directly to that literature. Exercise 1.3 will help you to do that.

EXERCISE 1.3

Writing a Purpose Statement

- ✓ Based on the grounding studies you discovered in your literature search for the first dissertation problem on your list, take a few minutes to write a purpose statement. [Note: The research study you propose must build directly on and extend the work of other scholars (Case D) or fill a gap (Case C) that you identified in the second step of the dissertation research process.]
- ✓ Repeat this step for each of your other high potential research topics.
- ✓ Set aside the problem statement, grounding literature summary, and purpose statement for each potential research topic and continue reading.

4. Research Questions (& Hypotheses)

Once you have identified the purpose for conducting your dissertation research project, you need to specify the questions you intend to answer with your study. These are your research questions, and they are very important.

What is a research question?

Basically, a research question indicates what you hope to learn from your study. There are two basic types of research questions—qualitative and quantitative.

If you want to learn the *what, why,* and *how* about your research topic, then you are asking qualitative research questions. Conversely, if you want to know the extent of the relationship (or the difference) between two or more variables, you are asking *how much* or quantitative research questions.

Here are a few examples of research questions:

A. How do employees cope with seemingly constant change in their work environment?

B. How much of an effect does leadership style have on follower satisfaction?

C. What are the factors that determine project success or failure?

D. Why do nurses sometimes feel abused by patients?

E. How much more effective is this new drug than the best existing one?

Can you determine which of these questions are qualitative and which are quantitative in nature?

A. If you want to know the answer to this question, you will need to ask the employees. From their answers, you will try to construct an explanation or theory of how they cope. [This type of theory construction based on inductive reasoning is the essence of *qualitative* research.]

B. In this case, you have two variables—an independent one (leadership style), and a dependent one (follower satisfaction). Your objective is to determine a mathematically valid relationship (i.e., a statistically significant correlation) between them based an existing theory that postulates a relationship between them. In effect, your study will test the hypothesis that such a relationship exists for your target population. [This type of theory/hypothesis testing based on deductive reasoning is the essence of *quantitative* research.]

C. Who best knows what factors affect project success? For your study, you will need to select a group of people (i.e., a purposefully selected sample of the people in the target population you are studying) whom you believe have the answers to your research question. They will most likely be people who have lived through successful and unsuccessful projects of the type that interests you, from the organization(s) which you intend to study. To make the results of your study more believable (i.e., valid), you might ask not only individual contributors who were involved, but also managers who lived through the project implementations as well, to see if both groups have the same views about what makes projects successful. [This effort to build a theory of project success is another example of *qualitative* research.]

D. As in cases A and C, to answer this question you will have to ask the nurses themselves; in particular, a sample of those who have experienced patient abuse. [Hence, a study of this kind would involve *qualitative* research.]

E. To test the efficacy of a new drug requires the strongest form of evidence. Therefore, if you want to answer this research question you will need to perform an experiment in which you measure and compare the effect of the new drug to that of the best existing alternative. Only experiments have the power to measure causal relationships, which is what you will need to demonstrate by means of your study to develop a strong enough case for replacing the existing drug with the new one. [Experimental research like this is *quantitative* research.]

While by no means exhaustive, this set of examples is representative. Hopefully, as a result of examining them you now have a good idea of the difference between research questions that lead to qualitative research (e.g., *what*, *why*, and *how* questions), and research questions best answered by quantitative research methods (e.g., *how much* questions).

EXERCISE 1.4a

Specifying Research Questions

- ✓ For the research idea on your list with the highest potential, write a list of the research questions that you wish to answer with your dissertation research. Be sure that each question addresses a single issue (like the sample questions), rather than multiple issues.
- ✓ Set aside your problem statement, grounding literature summary, purpose statement, and research questions for that idea.
- ✓ Repeat this process for each of your other potential research topics.
- ✓ Continue reading.

Hypotheses in Quantitative Research

In qualitative research, which generally involves some form of theory development, the research questions per se guide the investigation. However, in quantitative research, which generally involves testing one or more hypotheses derived from known (i.e., prior) theory, the hypotheses generated from the research questions guide the investigation.

To illustrate how to determine appropriate hypotheses from a quantitative research question (RQ), we will examine the two quantitative sample research questions (i.e., B and E).

RQ: *How much of an effect does leadership style have on follower satisfaction?*

H_0: Leadership style has no effect on follower satisfaction.

H_a: Leadership style has an effect on follower satisfaction.

H_0 and H_a are the null and alternative hypotheses, respectively, that correspond to this research question. The goal of a study with this research question would be to determine if there is sufficient statistical evidence to reject the null hypothesis (i.e., that there is no relationship between the two variables) in favor of the alternative hypothesis (i.e., that there is a statistically significant correlation between leadership style and follower satisfaction).

Can you figure out a set of appropriate hypotheses for sample question E?

RQ: *How much more effective is this new drug than the best existing one?*

H_0: The new drug is less than or equal to the best existing drug in effectiveness.

H_a: The new drug is more effective than the best existing drug.

H_0 and H_a are the null and alternative hypotheses, respectively, that correspond to this research question. The goal of a study with this research question would be to determine if there is sufficient statistical evidence to reject the null hypothesis (i.e., that the new drug is no more effective) in favor of the alternative hypothesis (i.e., that the new drug is better).

[Note: The set of hypotheses for sample research question E (called directional hypotheses) differ in from those for sample research question B (which are non-directional hypotheses). For more on how to develop appropriate hypotheses for quantitative research questions, see Appendix B.]

EXERCISE 1.4b

Specifying Hypotheses

- ✓ For each of the quantitative research questions for a given potential research topic on your list, create a null and an alternative hypothesis.
- ✓ Set aside your problem statement, grounding literature summary, purpose statement, research questions, and hypotheses (if any) for each potential research problem and continue reading.

We will have more to say about statistical significance and other aspects of hypothesis testing later, when we discuss research design. For now, it is sufficient to focus on the form of the hypotheses, not on how to test them.

5. Research Method

Now that you have defined your research questions (and related hypotheses if your research question is a quantitative one), you will need to choose a research method(s) that will enable you to answer those questions. Before you can do this, you will need to learn some things about the scientific method. Although we alluded to the scientific method in the previous section, it is important to take a few minutes now to examine it further.

The Scientific Method

Advocated by Sir Francis Bacon in the 17th century, the scientific method is most often associated with the natural sciences. It is, however, a generic approach to the creation of knowledge that applies equally to the social sciences. Simply stated, the scientific method is a two-step, systematic way of proceeding from facts to theories; and, if the theories hold up to repeated testing of hypotheses derived from them, eventually from theories to laws.

As shown in Figure 2, the first (*qualitative*) step involves gathering data based on specific observations and inferring from those facts more general propositions/axioms/theories that explain the observations. [Based on inductive reasoning, this is the theory building step.]

The second (*quantitative*) step involves deriving a hypothesis based on an existing theory, and testing it by means of previously collected (secondary) data or (primary) data collected from an experiment or survey expressly designed for the purposes of the study. [Based on deductive reasoning, this is the theory testing step.]

Qualitative Research Methods

Qualitative research methods—such as case study, grounded theory, phenomenology, ethnography, and action research—provide answers to qualitative research questions (e.g., what, why, and how). They involve the use of inductive methods to build a theory, or the elements of a theory, that explains the data collected from a purposive sample (i.e., chosen on purpose by the researcher) of participants who have experienced a phenomenon (such as those described earlier in sample research questions A, C, and D). [Note: To learn more about qualitative research methods, see Appendix C.]

A. Inductive: Theory Building/Qualitative (Specific to General)

B. Deductive: Theory Testing/Quantitative (General to Specific)

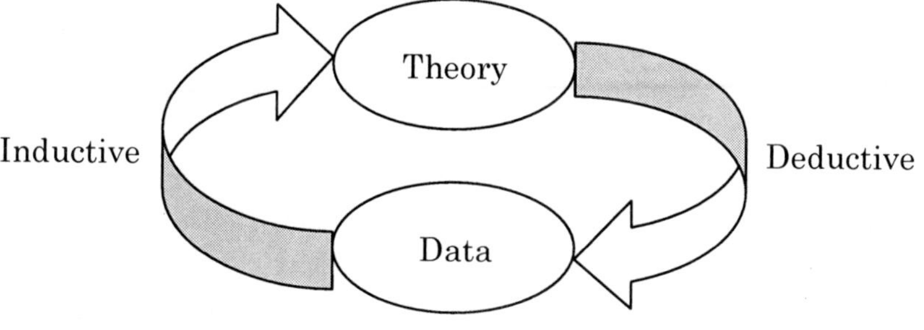

Figure 2. Scientific Method

Quantitative Research Methods

Quantitative research methods—such as an experiment, quasi-experiment, survey, existing data analysis, and meta-analysis (a special type of existing data analysis)—provide answers to quantitative research questions (e.g., relationship or difference questions such as those described earlier in sample research questions B and E). They involve the use of deductive methods to test hypotheses derived from theories using data collected from a representative sample of the target population chosen at random. The findings either support the theories or suggest the need to revise them. [Note: To learn more about quantitative research methods, see Appendix C.]

Mixed Methods Research

If you have both qualitative and quantitative research questions, then you must employ a combination of qualitative and quantitative methods in your dissertation research to answer them. This is a mixed methods study.

A mixed methods study might involve using qualitative research methods first to develop a theory, then using quantitative methods to test hypotheses based on that theory. Alternatively, it might involve first conducting an experiment, administering a survey, or analyzing existing data to test hypotheses derived from an existing theory, then using qualitative methods to develop further insight into the findings of the quantitative portion of the study.

EXERCISE 1.5

Selecting a Research Method

- ✓ For each of the potential research topics on your list, determine, based on your research questions, whether you will need to use qualitative or quantitative research methods (or both) to answer them.
- ✓ Set aside your problem statement, grounding literature summary, purpose statement, research questions and hypotheses (if any), and choice of quantitative or qualitative research method for addressing each potential research problem and continue reading.

6. Research Design

In this stage of the dissertation research process, you define the essential elements of your research design. To illustrate how to do this, we will first examine the research design elements for a hypothetical quantitative study, then for a hypothetical qualitative study.

Quantitative Research Design

For a quantitative study, the essential elements of your research design will include the following:

- ✓ the variables you will study,
- ✓ the assumed relationship between those variables,
- ✓ the alternative research methods you considered,

- ✓ the research method you selected and why,
- ✓ the target population you intend to study,
- ✓ how you will select the sample of study participants,
- ✓ how you will measure your variables,
- ✓ how you will collect your data in a way that ensures its validity and reliability,
- ✓ how you will analyze that data to arrive at statistically meaningful conclusions about your hypotheses (and thus answers to the corresponding research questions), and
- ✓ how you will protect the rights of study participants during the process of collecting and analyzing your data, as well as disseminating your findings.

The first step in designing the research for a quantitative study is to specify which variables you are studying and how they are related. For example, you may be interested in the connection, if any, between project manager leadership style and project success. Based on prior research, you know that there is evidence in the leadership literature to support a relationship between leadership style and the organizational performance; namely, that modern, collaborative leadership styles (like transformational leadership, charismatic leadership, and visionary leadership) tend to result in higher levels of employee performance, satisfaction, trust, and loyalty. Based on your personal experience, you believe that this generic finding might be true for project managers and project success. Hence, you decide to study the relationship between project manager leadership style (the independent variable) and project success (the dependent variable). [Note: All quantitative dissertation studies must have at least one independent and one dependent variable, and must measure a presumed relationship between them. For more on developing the underlying model for your study, see Appendix D.]

To study this relationship, you could (a) use existing data (if you were lucky enough to find some that dealt with this relationship for these specific variables), (b) design a controlled experiment (which would probably be difficult if not impossible to do given the realities of project management), or (c) use a survey instrument to collect data on project manager leadership style and project success. The last alternative, a survey, seems doable for most doctoral student; the other two generally do not.

Now that you know what you want to study and what research method you will use, you need to determine your target population. The target population is a subset of the general population (which is all project managers in this hypothetical study) that you can reasonably expect to include in your study. Then you will need to identify a sampling frame from which to select a sample from that target population.

If you could gain access to a group of project managers, you could ask them in your survey instrument about their leadership style and the success of their projects. One way to do gain access to a target population of project managers, particularly if you were a member, would be to approach a project management association and ask them if they were interested in your study and would give you access to their membership list. If they were, then you would have the means to develop a sampling frame (essentially a representative listing of your target population) from which you could draw a random sample. [Note: Random sampling from a representative sampling frame of the target population is a requirement for a quantitative study because statistical methods used to generalize sample findings to the larger population assume that the sample is random and representative. See Appendix E for more on sampling.]

The responses you received from a random sample of project managers would provide you with data needed to measure the correlation between project manager leadership style and project success. [Note: You would need to continue to collect responses until your sample was equal to or greater than the minimum required sample size—the estimated number of responses required to obtain a statistically significant relationship between the two variables under certain predetermined conditions that we will discuss later.] If you could also gain access to people who worked on the projects with the managers and get their opinions of the managers' leadership styles and the success of those projects, you could compare what they said to what the project managers said, thus strengthening your study. If you could get hold of some hard data on project success, analyzing it would strengthen your study even more. The name for this process of strengthening a study by analyzing data from different sources and comparing the findings of each separate analysis is triangulation.

How you choose to measure each of the variables in your quantitative study will have a major impact on the validity of your findings. To measure project manager leadership style, you could (a) design a questionnaire of your own in which you ask each participant to select his or her leadership style from a list of styles you provide, or (b) use a published instrument specifically designed to measure leadership style. While the former might seem easier and less expensive (if there is a charge for using the published instrument), the likelihood of obtaining an accurate assessment of each participant's true leadership style is much greater if they answer a series of questions built into a published instrument in a way that maximizes the validity and reliability of the resulting measurement of leadership style than if each project manager simply selects from a list of styles that you provide in a survey of your own design.

To measure project success, you could (a) ask the project managers to describe and rate the success of specific projects they managed, (b) ask participants in these projects to describe and rate the success of each project, (c) ask the managers of the project managers to describe and rate the success of the projects, or (d) obtain hard data on project success (if available) as measured by return on investment or some other standard business metric. As you can imagine, any of the latter three approaches, or some combination of the four, would probably yield better data than the first approach. However, issues of time, cost, and access might make the first approach more doable for you as a doctoral student, and still provide you with valid data for your study. The challenge would then be to design a second survey instrument, based on the existing literature on project success, that would enable you to collect meaningful (i.e., valid and reliable) data from each project manager who participates in the study about the degree to which his or her projects have succeeded. Each participant would complete and submit both this questionnaire on project success and the first instrument on leadership style.

Prior to sending out your surveys (either by mail or by email invitation to participate in an online survey), you would determine the minimum required sample size to provide sufficient data to estimate the correlation between project manager leadership style and project success with a predetermined likelihood of obtaining statistically significant results. You would continue to collect responses until you had received a number of fully completed, usable surveys at least equal to that minimum sample size. You would not have to restrict yourself to this number of responses, but you would need to have at least this many surveys before you stop collecting and start analyzing your data.

For the sake of discussion, let us assume that the minimum sample size was 80, and that you received 110 responses from participants, which, after eliminating those with missing data, left you with 100 usable surveys. From your analysis of each of the two surveys completed by the project managers who participated in your study, you arrived at a single measure of leadership style, and a corresponding single measure of project success, for each participant. By entering this data into SPSS or some other statistical program, which does the laborious computations for you, you determine the correlation between your independent and dependent variables and the probability that such a correlation could occur by chance. You hope to be able, based on the correlation between your two key variables, to reject the null hypothesis that there is no relationship between project manager leadership style and project success in favor of the alternative hypothesis that there is a relationship. If you chose a level of significance for your hypothesis test of 5% (which is the standard choice), and the correlation computed by the statistical program has a p-value (i.e., probability that it could occur by chance) of less than or equal to 5%, then you can reject the null hypothesis. Otherwise, you cannot. Either way, you have achieved your objective of measuring the relationship between project manager leadership style and project success based on the limitations inherent in your choice of target population, your sampling scheme, and your ability to measure each variable.

Finally, as a researcher you have an ethical responsibility to protect the rights of and not harm the participants in your study. To prevent this from happening, you will have to design your dissertation research in such a way that it passes the test of a rigorous review by your university's institutional review board (IRB) *before* you receive permission to collect your data. We will discuss this part of the dissertation review process in more detail later in the chapter on writing the formal proposal for your research project.

EXERCISE 1.6a

Specifying Key Elements of a Quantitative Research Design

✓ For the highest priority potential research topics on your list, specify each of the essential elements of a quantitative research project designed to study it.

✓ For that topic, your problem statement, grounding literature summary, purpose statement, research questions and hypotheses (if any), choice of quantitative or qualitative research method(s), and key research design elements collectively constitute an integrated research plan (IRP) in the sense that all of the six parts are aligned. Although subject to refinement as you continue to work on your dissertation, because of the systematic process you followed in developing it, the six components of your IRP form the basis of a coherent, systemic, integrated plan for a dissertation research project to address your topic.

✓ If you wish, you may develop IRPs for the second or third highest priority topics on your list of research topics, but that is not necessary if you are now convinced that you have identified and specified how you would approach, by means of your integrated research plan for it, *the* topic you want to study for your dissertation.

✓ Set aside the IRP(s) for your highest priority topic(s) and continue reading.

Qualitative Research Design

For qualitative studies, the essential elements of your research design will include the following:

- ✓ the case, idea, or phenomenon that you intend to study,
- ✓ the alternative research methods you considered,
- ✓ the research method you selected and why,
- ✓ the nature of the target population you intend to study,
- ✓ how you will select your sample of study participants,
- ✓ whether you will use multiple sources of information (triangulation) to enhance the validity and believability of your study, and which sources you will use,
- ✓ how you will collect and analyze your data,
- ✓ your role as a researcher in the data collection process, and
- ✓ how you will protect the rights of study participants during the process of collecting and analyzing your data, as well as disseminating your findings.

The first step in designing the research for a qualitative study is to identify a case, idea, or phenomenon that you intend to study. For example, you may be interested in the phenomenon of patient abuse of nurses. Based on prior research, you realize that little is known about this phenomenon, despite the fact that you have seen it happen on numerous occasions and have heard several nurse friends of yours discussing its detrimental impact, particularly on new nurses. Fortunately, you have discovered a doctoral dissertation on the subject, which will serve as the grounding study for your research project.

To answer your research questions, which focus on what, when, where, why, how, and to whom it happens, as well as what might be done to prevent it or limit its consequences when it does, you could (a) select a specific site, such as a hospital, and use a case study approach to help you identify, collect, analyze, interpret, and compare qualitative/subjective data (from interviews with nurses, administrators, and others in that bounded system who have insight into the phenomenon, and from content analysis of formal documents) with quantitative/hard data (such as frequency measures for reported cases of patient abuse of nurses, and statistics on nurse turnover). Alternatively, you could (b) select a group of nurses, administrators, and others with insight into the phenomenon from several hospitals or other health care facilities and use grounded theory to help you develop insights into the phenomenon based on in-depth interviews using the constant comparative method of data collection and analysis (more on this later). Finally, you could (c) select a sample of nurses whose patients have abused them (i.e., a purposive sample) and interview them in great depth about their experiences using a phenomenological research method. [Note: For more on selecting a sample in a qualitative research project, see Appendix E.]

Any of these approaches could be suitable for a dissertation research project, as would other variations on these three alternatives—such as using phenomenological methods in case b or grounded theory in case c. Your choice would depend on a number of factors. For example, if you were primarily interested in patient abuse of nurses at a given facility, you would choose the case study approach and collect data on the phenomenon from a number of different sources within that facility so that you could compare and contrast (i.e., triangulate) what you learn from each. This would increase the likelihood of arriving at valid findings for the phenomenon at that particular health care facility.

Alternatively, if you were more interested in exploring the general phenomenon than the facility, you would probably choose a grounded theory or a phenomenological approach. If you wanted to explore in the greatest possible depth the perspective of nurses who had suffered from patient abuse, you would select a purposive sample of such nurses to study (as in case c). If you were interested in other views on the phenomenon, perhaps because you wanted to determine if they also saw it as a serious problem, you would collect and analyze data from administrators and people other than the nurses themselves who were familiar enough with the phenomenon to provide valid insights (such as in case b).

There are two primary ways to collect and analyze data. In quantitative research, data collection is the first step, and data analysis is the second step. For example, you send out a survey to potential respondents and when you have at least the minimum number of completed, usable surveys in hand, you code, edit (as necessary), and analyze the data. In qualitative research, data collection and analysis occur in a much more interactive fashion. Analysis of initial data collected from early interviews with study participants informs the direction of a subsequent round of interviews, the analysis of which informs the direction of yet another round of interviews, and so forth. This iterative process continues until no major insights other than those already discovered emerge. Reaching this point in the joint data collection, coding, and analysis process—the saturation point—signals that it is time to stop collecting data. In practice, this often occurs after 10 or 15 interviews with a group of similar participants, such as the abused nurses in the phenomenological study (case c), or the administrators in the grounded theory study (case b). This method of qualitative data collection and analysis is the constant comparative method (Glaser & Strauss, 1967/2009).

Because the collection of qualitative data will require that you become directly involved in the process (e.g., by observing, interviewing, leading focus groups, or even participating), you must be clear about your role and you must ensure that the participants are aware of what it is. Furthermore, you must do your best to remain in that role throughout the study. This may be easier to say than do. For example, if in your role of observer or interviewer you discover that you know something that would be helpful to the participants in solving a problem they are dealing with, you must resist the temptation to become a participant by sharing that information.

Finally, as a researcher you have an ethical responsibility to protect the rights of and not harm the participants in your study. To prevent this from happening, you will have to design your dissertation research in such a way that it passes the test of a rigorous review by your university's institutional review board (IRB) *before* you receive permission to collect your data. We will discuss this process in more detail later in the chapter on writing the formal proposal for your research project.

EXERCISE 1.6b

Specifying Key Elements of a Qualitative Research Design

✓ For the highest priority potential research topics on your list, specify each of the essential elements of a qualitative research project designed to study it.

✓ For that topic, your problem statement, grounding literature summary, purpose statement, research questions and hypotheses (if any), choice of quantitative or qualitative research method(s), and key research design elements collectively constitute an integrated research plan (IRP).

Although subject to refinement as you continue to work on your dissertation, because of the systematic process you followed in developing it, the six components of your IRP form the basis of a coherent, systemic, integrated plan for a dissertation research project to address your topic.

✓ If you wish, you may develop IRPs for the second or third highest priority topics on your list of research topics, but that is not necessary if you are now convinced that you have identified and specified how you would approach, by means of your integrated research plan for it, *the* topic you want to study for your dissertation.

✓ Set aside the IRP(s) for your highest priority topic(s) and continue reading.

Mixed Methods Research Design

Because a mixed methods study is a composite of a quantitative and a qualitative study, it is necessary to develop a research design that has two parts. One part of the design addresses the quantitative research questions (and hypotheses), and the other addresses the qualitative research questions. The resulting integrated research plan consists of five joint components [i.e., problem statement, grounding literature summary, purpose statement, research questions and hypotheses (for each quantitative question), and a specification of the quantitative or qualitative research method(s) to address each research question], and a two-part research design component. For a quantitative study that will lead into a qualitative study, the research design component of the mixed methods IRP first (a) specifies the essential elements of the research design for the quantitative part of the study (addressing the issues raised earlier in the section on quantitative research design), and then (b) specifies the essential elements of the research design for the qualitative part of the study (addressing the issues raised earlier in the section on qualitative research design). If the qualitative study will lead into the quantitative study, present the qualitative research design in your IRP before your present the quantitative design.

EXERCISE 1.6c

Specifying Key Elements of a Mixed Methods Research Design

✓ Follow the instructions in the quantitative research design section to develop the elements of a research design for addressing the quantitative research questions associated with your highest priority research topic. Follow the instructions in the qualitative research design section to develop the elements of a research design for addressing the qualitative research questions associated with your highest priority research topic. Include both in the final section of your IRP.

✓ If you wish, you may develop IRPs for the second or third highest priority topics on your list of research topics, but that is not necessary if you are now convinced that you have identified and specified how you would approach, by means of your integrated research plan for it, *the* topic you want to study for your dissertation.

✓ Set aside the IRP(s) for your highest priority topic(s) and continue reading.

Integrated Research Plan (IRP)

Congratulations on completing your integrated research plan! To reiterate, the IRP for your chosen dissertation topic consists of six parts:

1. Your *problem* statement
2. A *grounding literature* summary
3. A *purpose* statement
4. *Research questions*, and hypotheses (if any),
5. Quantitative or qualitative *research method*(s) you have selected to enable you to answer the research questions and test the hypotheses (if any)
6. Key elements of your *research design*

As shown in Table 2, the IRP is the result of addressing each of the first six steps in the dissertation research process in the sequential, systemic, iterative manner described earlier in this chapter to develop a coherent plan for your research. The development of the IRP precedes the writing of the dissertation proposal.

Table 2. Principal Output of the Dissertation Research Process

#	Step	Output
1	Problem	
2	Grounding Literature	
3	Purpose	
4	Research Questions	
5	Research Method	
6	Research Design	Integrated Research Plan
7	Proposal	
8	Research	
9	Dissertation	Dissertation
10	Publication	Journal Articles & Books

The completion of an integrated research plan and its approval by your dissertation committee chair is a crucial step in your dissertation journey. It may take as little as a week or as much as a month (and perhaps even a bit longer) to complete your IRP, but it is time very well invested. Without it, the vast majority of students flounder, wasting valuable time/money writing a proposal that will never gain approval by a dissertation committee without substantial revision because it lacks one or more of the essential elements of an IRP or because the parts don't align (i.e., don't fit together logically and coherently).

For example, a student proposes a study to solve an important real world problem, but suggests an approach that does not build on (i.e., is not grounded in) the existing research literature, thus making it unacceptable. Or, she wants to know why something (i.e., a phenomenon) happens (which will require theory building/qualitative research), but proposes to get the answers by means of a quantitative study (which is a way of testing existing theory). Or, he proposes to study a particular group or organization (to which he has access) as a specific example of a more general situation or phenomenon, without realizing that he cannot generalize his findings from this qualitative case study to a broader population, which he insists on being able to do. Or, she proposes to do a quantitative, survey-based study to test for a relationship between an independent and a dependent variable that is based on conjecture alone (i.e., for which no theory exists in the literature), instead of the qualitative (theory building) study called for, because she is more comfortable with quantitative data analysis.

Situations in which the preferred research method drives the proposed study, instead of the research questions leading to the choice of appropriate research method(s), also manifest themselves in proposals to do qualitative studies without including relevant numerical data analysis, or in lieu of preferable quantitative studies, because a student is not comfortable with statistics. These are just a few examples of situations that may result in a student having to rewrite a proposal extensively, or even start over with a new topic, because he or she failed to invest the time to develop and gain approval for a solid IRP. Suffice it to say that not taking the time to develop an IRP is a big mistake that you should avoid making.

Now that you have thought deeply enough about the nature of your dissertation research to create an integrated research plan for it, you have the core or backbone of your dissertation figured out. When someone asks you about your dissertation, you can provide a simple, confident, clear, and logical explanation of what you intend to study, and how you plan to study it. When you start writing your dissertation, you have the essence of the first three chapters (i.e., the proposal) neatly and logically summarized in your ten to twenty page IRP to guide you. You have completed the first phase of your dissertation journey.

7. Proposal

What is a dissertation? As stated in an earlier chapter, a dissertation is a scholarly report, generally consisting of five chapters that provide (a) an overview of a research project, (b) a review of relevant literature, (c) a detailed description of the research methods used, (d) an explanation of the results obtained, and (e) the conclusions drawn from these findings as well as recommendations for professional application and further study.

What is a proposal? The proposal is the first three chapters of the dissertation written in anticipation of receiving permission to conduct the research project it proposes. Hence, it contains (a) an overview of the research project (in Chapter 1), (b) a review of relevant literature (in Chapter 2), and (c) a detailed description (in Chapter 3) of the research method(s) you propose to use to conduct your study and how you will apply the method(s). The proposal is, in effect, a formal, detailed plan for conducting your research.

As shown in Table 3, the six parts of the IRP directly affect each chapter in the proposal to varying degrees. [Note that P = Primary effect, S = Secondary effect, and T = Tertiary effect.]

Table 3. How the IRP informs the Proposal

		Chapter		
#	**IRP Step**	**1**	**2**	**3**
1	Problem	P	T	S
2	Grounding Literature	P	S	T
3	Purpose	P	T	S
4	Research Questions	P	T	S
5	Research Method	P	T	S
6	Research Design	P	T	S

We will examine in some detail the required content of each chapter of the proposal in a later chapter. For now, simply note, as Table 3 suggests, that a properly developed, coherent IRP greatly influences and facilitates the writing of the proposal.

Another important document, related to the proposal, that you must write and submit to your university for approval of your study, is the application you must make to the university's Institutional Review Board (IRB). The IRB reviews each proposed research project from an ethical and research perspective to determine whether or not it has the potential to harm participants in the study. Issues identified as problematic by the IRB require revision to the proposal until it meets with IRB approval. We will cover the purpose and procedures of the IRB in more detail in the chapter on writing the proposal.

8. Research

Once you receive approval from the university to conduct your proposed study (which confirms the quality of your proposed research plan), and from the IRB (which confirms its ethical soundness), you are free to conduct your research. [Note: To protect potential study participants, IRB rules forbid the collection of study data in advance of IRB approval. Exceptions to this rule are not made, and violations are dealt with severely (e.g., by invalidating the data, or worse).] This will involve collecting, editing (as necessary), and analyzing your data in the precise manner that you have described in your proposal. [Note: If deviations from your proposal are necessary to deal with unforeseen difficulties, then you will need to document them in your dissertation to preserve its integrity as a record of what you proposed to study, how you conducted your research, what you discovered, and what it means for researchers and practitioners.]

We will examine issues associated with conducting dissertation research in considerable detail in Part II.

9. Dissertation

When you have completed your data collection and analysis, you will need to present your findings relative to each of your research questions (and hypotheses, if any) in the final two chapters of your dissertation (as shown in Table 4). In Part II, we will examine issues associated with writing these last two chapters of the dissertation.

Table 4. Dissertation Chapters

#	Chapter	Description
1	Introduction	Overview of essential aspects of the study
2	Literature Review	Review of relevant literature to produce a theoretical foundation for the study
3	Research Method	Description of research method(s) and design
4	Results	Description of findings relative to the research questions (and hypotheses)
5	Conclusions and Recommendations	Interpretation of the findings Significance of the study Implications for practice Recommendations for more research

10. Publication

When you reach this point, the tenth and last step in the dissertation research process, you have come a long way. As a result, you owe it to yourself and others who might benefit from a wider dissemination of the research findings from your dissertation to publish them in a number of academic and professional outlets, such as respected, peer-reviewed journals, as stand-alone books or chapters in an edited collection on your topic, or in the proceedings of conferences where you choose to present. We will have more to say about the important publication process in Part II.

Chapter 4

What is the Dissertation Review Process?

The dissertation review process and the dissertation research process are similar, but not identical. While the dissertation review process contains many of the steps in the dissertation research process, it does not include certain crucial ones (such as the development of a solid IRP), which leads to major problems for some doctoral students (ranging from more frequent and substantial revisions to the ultimate penalty of failure to gain approval for the dissertation research). In addition, because the dissertation must meet the university's standards for a demonstration of a doctoral student's ability to design, conduct, and report the findings of a research project, the dissertation review process contains many checkpoints (at which various university scholars assess the proposal/dissertation) that are not inherent to the dissertation research process. These additional steps include reviews by the chair, the full committee, university research scholars, university writing center personnel, the institutional review board (IRB), and the chief academic officer (CAO) of the university (or the equivalent).

The similarities and differences between the two processes are evident from an inspection of Table 5, which shows the 10 steps of the dissertation research process in the first column and the most common steps in the dissertation review process in the second column.

Table 5. Review Process vs. Research Process

Dissertation Research	Dissertation Review
IRP (Steps 1–6)	Prospectus (Pre-Proposal)
Proposal (Step 7)	Proposal
	Proposal Oral (if required)
	IRB
Research (Step 8)	Research
Dissertation (Step 9)	Dissertation
	Dissertation Oral
Publication (Step 10)	

Another step in the dissertation research process that is generally not in the dissertation review process is the final one—publication. Because the review process ends with the acceptance of the dissertation (based primarily on the final oral defense), many students, without the academic support provided by the committee and other university resources during the review process, do not know how to publish their work, and hence fail to do so. Do not let this happen to you. Follow the advice in Chapter 8 to improve the chances of publishing your findings.

The university checkpoints alluded to earlier occur in different places in the review process at different universities. Common checkpoints include committee, university research expert, and IRB reviews prior to the acceptance of the proposal; and committee, university research expert, writing center, and chief academic officer reviews prior to acceptance of the dissertation.

Finally, some schools require an oral defense at the proposal stage as well as the dissertation stage; while others only require that the student defend his or her dissertation in an oral held near the end of the review process.

[Note: This overview of the dissertation review process is for the sake of illustration. It does not and cannot include every variation on the process for every university. It is your responsibility as doctoral student to discover and prepare yourself for the unique requirements of your university's review process.]

Part II

Dissertation Writing

Chapter 5

Writing the Proposal

The secret to writing a first class proposal and dissertation is simple. First, develop a solid integrated research plan (IRP), one that can stand up to the scrutiny of your committee chair and others (e.g., fellow doctoral students, friends who have a doctorate, etc.), *before* you write a single word. Second, follow your university's dissertation rubric and other dissertation guidelines to the letter. Third, write like a scholar.

Develop a Solid IRP

In Part I, you developed a coherent IRP for your dissertation research based on the information and exercises provided to you. Before you begin writing your proposal, you should develop a simple explanation of your research (i.e., an "elevator speech") based on your IRP that you can use to answer the question: "What is your dissertation about?" This is the acid test of your IRP. If it meets with your chair's approval and you can articulate what you intend to do, why, and how briefly and coherently to anyone else who asks, your IRP passes the test and will serve admirably as the core of your proposal and dissertation, as shown in Figure 3.

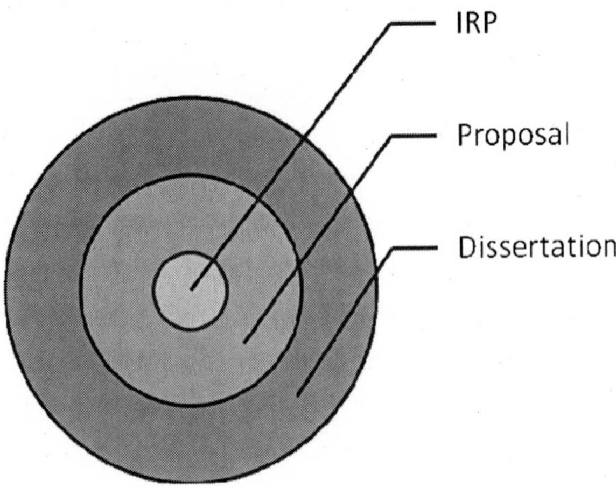

Figure 3. Relationship of IRP to Proposal and Dissertation

Follow the Rubric and Template

As you will learn later in this chapter, a solid IRP provides essential content required to address many of the issues that a well written proposal and dissertation must answer. For now, suffice it to say that you should follow the dissertation rubric/guidelines provided by your university to the letter! If the rubric specifies the title of each section (e.g., Problem Statement), those are the titles you should use. Don't make up your own titles (e.g., Statement of the Problem), and don't include additional sections unless the rubric does not cover an area that is vital to your proposal or dissertation. If the rubric prescribes the sequence for each of the required sections (e.g., Problem Statement, Research Questions, Purpose Statement), then follow that sequence. Don't make your own sequence (e.g., Purpose Statement, Problem Statement, Research Questions).

In the same vein, if the rubric specifies the content of a section, then provide information germane to your proposed research that addresses the content requirements of that section. Do not add content that the rubric specifies belongs in other areas of the proposal, and do not leave out required information for that section. Of course, if a section specified in the rubric does not pertain to your study, then leave it out of your proposal. Conversely, if your study requires a section not specified in the rubric, insert it in a logical place. Finally, note that because of their central role in the methodology of every research project, the research questions (and the hypotheses for a quantitative study) serve as an important focus of the proposal and dissertation. For example, rubrics for Chapter 4 of the dissertation (in which you explain the results of the study) generally specify that you organize this chapter by research question and report your findings in relation to each one. To reiterate, *follow the guidelines for the sections of the rubric that pertain to your unique dissertation research project to the letter*!

Just as the dissertation rubric covers the required *content* for the proposal and dissertation, the dissertation template covers the required *formatting* of these documents. You cannot make up your own formatting. Generally created by the writing center staff or other experts in form and style, a dissertation template contains the proper margins, spacing, fonts, section headings, sequencing of required content, and the like for the proposal and dissertation. You will save yourself much revision time, and convey a much more scholarly impression to readers of your work, if you use the template from the outset to *ensure that your proposal or dissertation meets the formatting requirements specified in the dissertation template.* [Note: Some students rely on special software designed to help with APA style to keep track of their in-text and reference citations. Information added to the proposal or dissertation by copying and pasting from the software's files is often not in the correct font or font size, and, more importantly, is sometimes not consistent with current APA style requirements. It is your responsibility to review these insertions to make sure that they meet the formatting requirements built into the template, which includes being in correct APA style.]

Write like a Scholar

If you want to impress your committee and other university reviewers, and as a result dramatically reduce the time it takes to complete your proposal and dissertation, write like a scholar from day one. Scholars write with an eye to both content and form. They know that great ideas poorly expressed will not impress reviewers any more than will poor ideas beautifully expressed. So they strive to express their good ideas in simple, correct English and in proper APA style (or the equivalent style required by the university).

Demonstrate Higher Order Critical Thinking

Expressing the critical thinking that has gone into your prior research, and which you have summarized in your IRP, is essential to conveying the quality of your ideas (i.e., your content). The higher order critical thinking required of you and all doctoral students, per Bloom (1956), focuses on analysis, synthesis, and evaluation of other scholars' ideas, rather than the lower order critical thinking typical of masters and undergraduate level work, which emphasizes description and straightforward application of the ideas. [Note: Google *Bloom's Taxonomy* to learn more about the difference between lower and higher order critical thinking.]

Apply the BOAT Principle

Write in a balanced, objective, accurate, and tentative (BOAT) manner (Levasseur, 2006). Present both sides of an issue as accurately as possible in a way that makes the point based on the preponderance of evidence available, rather than leaving out conflicting evidence (which suggests bias, something that always exists but is your responsibility to manage). And offer your conclusions tentatively; they depend on the quality and strength of the evidence that supports them, which may change as new, perhaps contradictory, findings emerge from the ongoing process of academic research. This type of writing, which relies on the quality and presentation of evidence to influence readers, is the opposite of the way some doctoral students have learned to write, which is to present ideas in a one-sided manner supported by personal experience and opinion in an attempt to convince the reader by the sheer force of the arguments they make. Avoid the latter in favor of the BOAT principle.

Adhere to Form and Style Rules

Do your very best to submit work that follows the rules of good English (Strunk & White, 1979) and adheres to APA style requirements (American Psychological Association, 2010) every time. Based on my experience as the chair, content expert, or methodologist on numerous dissertation committees, this is the second most problematic area in most proposals, surpassed only by the troubles caused by the absence of a coherent IRP. Perhaps this is because learning APA is so much like learning a foreign language that students avoid doing it. However, because the latest APA publication manual (American Psychological Association, 2010) is so much easier to use than earlier editions were for most of my students, I insist that all my mentees read the manual from cover to cover and use it as a guide to their dissertation work and its ultimate publication, rather than treating the manual like an encyclopedia or other reference work and referring to it only for the answers to specific questions. I strongly urge you to do the same thing.

Demonstrating higher order critical thinking skills, applying the BOAT principle, and adhering to form and style rules are some of the most important things to do to write like a scholar. In contrast, here are a few specific things to avoid.

First, use the first person sparingly, and only to express actions that you as the researcher in your dissertation study will do (e.g., I will interview 15 people). Otherwise, write in the third person. Your personal opinions do not belong in a dissertation.

Second, write in the active voice, not the passive voice. No one would say something like, "A curve ball was thrown by the pitcher for a strike" to describe an action they witnessed. Rather, he or she would say, "The pitcher threw a curve ball for a strike." Yet academic writing is full of such obscure sentences. Avoid them at all costs by writing in the third person, active voice, except on those occasions when the first person is more appropriate.

Third, avoid personifying objects or abstractions. Students often write phrases like "This chapter will analyze" when what they mean is that they will present an analysis in the chapter. The chapter, which is not a person, cannot analyze anything. This is an example of personification or anthropomorphism. A better way to the say the same thing would be, "This chapter will include an analysis of" followed by the subject of the analysis.

Fourth, avoid filler or redundancy. The proposal and dissertation do not have to be tomes. So, do not add extra material or repeat previously stated material (with the exception of the Research Questions and Hypotheses, and similar material specified in the rubric that must be consistent from chapter to chapter) just to add more pages to your document.

Finally, to avoid plagiarizing, some students will rely extensively on direct quotations from the authors of the works they cite as evidence to support their arguments. This practice is in fact a violation of academic integrity in the sense that the resulting document is essentially not their work, but a composite of other scholars' ideas. To counteract this tendency, most universities have guidelines that limit the percentage of text that can consist of direct quotations (e.g., to less than 10%). You should learn to paraphrase properly (i.e., in your own words, with an appropriate in-text citation) to avoid this problem.

Express Your Scholarly Voice

Another important area to focus on to improve the quality of your proposal and dissertation is to write in your unique scholarly voice. Before explaining what this means let me deal with one common misconception about it. Scholars do not voice their unsubstantiated opinions directly in their writing. So, expressions like "I believe that" or "In my opinion" have no place in your proposal or dissertation. On the contrary, you must support every argument you make in your proposal that is not common sense or common knowledge with a reference to evidence in the literature.

Your scholarly voice is evident indirectly but clearly to the knowledgeable academic reader from the way in which you present and analyze the evidence in support of each point you make. Think of yourself as the moderator of a panel of experts on your dissertation topic. The audience for the panel discussion is not interested in what you have to say per se. Instead, they want to know what the experts think about each of the relevant aspects of the topic. So you raise each of those aspects and provide evidence from each of the experts, which you proceed to analyze (i.e., compare similarities, contrast differences), synthesize, and evaluate. Although you never say "I" in the process of doing this, your scholarly voice is evident to the reader based on the topics you choose, the evidence you select to support your arguments, and the way in which you critically assess that evidence.

Know the Proposal Structure

Now that you know the secret to writing a first class proposal and dissertation, we can turn our attention to the structure of each of these related documents. The proposal, which is a description of what you intend to do for your dissertation research if your university gives you permission, generally consists of (a) preliminary pages (e.g., title page, abstract, dedications, acknowledgements, table of contents, list of tables, and list of figures), (b) Chapters 1 to 3 (which, as shown previously in Table 4, cover the introduction to the study, literature review, and research method, respectively), (c) references, (d) appendices, and (e) curriculum vitae. The dissertation, which is a report of what you planned to do (Chapters 1, 2, and 3), what happened when you did it (Chapter 4), and what it all means (Chapter 5), consists of the proposal (with tenses in the abstract and Chapters 1 to 3 revised as necessary to reflect the fact that what you planned to do you have now done), with revisions if any to Chapters 1 and 3 to reflect differences in what you did versus what you planned to do, and with additional tables, figures, and appendices (if necessary) plus Chapters 4 and 5, and any other university required dissertation elements not included in the proposal.

To help you remember the parts of a typical proposal and dissertation, Table 6 lists them in order.

Table 6. Proposal and Dissertation Structure

Content	Proposal	Dissertation
Preliminary Pages:	x	x
Title Page	x	x
Abstract	x	x
Table of Contents	x	x
List of Tables	x	x
List of Figures	x	x
Chapter 1: Introduction	x	x
Chapter 2: Literature Review	x	x
Chapter 3: Research Method	x	x
Chapter 4: Results		x
Chapter 5: Conclusions and Recommendations		x
References	x	x
Appendices	x	x

Of course, this list is only suggestive. You will need to follow your university's proposal and dissertation template, which may require different content, when writing your documents.

Provide the Required Content

This section contains suggestions for enhancing the quality of each part of the proposal shown in Table 6. You will find similar information on Chapters 4 and 5 in the section on writing the dissertation.

Title

The title of your proposal/dissertation should be no more than 15 words in length and convey to the reader, directly or indirectly, (a) whether your research is quantitative or qualitative, (b) the variables or phenomena you are studying, and (c) and, if it is unusual, the specific methodology you will use (e.g., meta-analysis, narrative inquiry). Here are some examples of the titles of dissertations that meet these criteria. See if you can tell which of them are for qualitative studies and which are for quantitative ones. [Note: Mixed methods studies usually contain the words "mixed methods" somewhere in the title; generally as part of a subtitle following and separated by a colon from the main title.]

A. Creating Sustainable Change: A Grounded Theory Approach (Bezzubetz, 2009)

B. Assessing the Effects of Transshipments on Profit in a Two-Echelon Supply Chain (Greenburg, 2010)

C. Information Technology-Enabled Change Management: An Investigation of Individual Experiences (Gouker, 2009)

D. The Influence of Spirituality on Servant Leadership Among Small Business Entrepreneurs (Franklin, 2010)

E. The Impact of a Transforming Leadership Style on Follower Performance and Satisfaction: A Meta-Analysis (Levasseur, 2004)

F. A Historical Analysis of the Relationship Between Charisma and the Making of Great Leaders (Schilling, 2010)

If you identified A, C, and F as the titles of qualitative dissertations, and B, D, and E as the titles of quantitative dissertations, you were correct. Words like *grounded theory* (a qualitative research method) in title A, *investigation of individual experiences* in title C, and *historical analysis* (a qualitative research method) in title F indicate that the study is qualitative in nature. Similarly, words like *assessing the effects of (an independent variable) on (a dependent variable)* in title B, and *the influence* (or *impact*) *of (an independent variable) on (a dependent variable)* in title D (and title E) indicate that the study is quantitative in nature.

Abstract

As it is essentially a summary of your work, the abstract is a very important part of any dissertation. Hence, you must write your abstract with great attention to its accuracy, formatting, and representativeness of your actual study, following the rubric and any special abstract guidelines provided by your university as carefully as possible. Think of it as a marketing piece for your study; an integral part of your work that is also capable of serving as the stand alone document that others will read to decide if your dissertation is worth reading in more depth.

Typical guidelines (a) restrict the abstract to one page, (b) require that it be one continuous paragraph, and (c) dictate its content—problem, theoretical foundation, purpose, research questions, research methodology, population, participants, data collection and analysis techniques, findings, conclusions and recommendations, and social significance.

Because of its importance, the abstract receives a careful examination at each step of the dissertation review process, culminating with an assessment by the highest level university representative responsible for approving the dissertation (e.g., the Chief Academic Officer). So, write your abstract with care the first time (in the proposal stage), and continue to polish it based on the feedback you receive from your committee and university reviewers until it is as good as you can possibly make it.

Tables of Contents/Lists of Tables and Figures

Adhere to the proposal/dissertation template formatting exactly when creating your table of contents and your lists of tables and figures. If you use your word processing software to create your table of contents for you, be especially careful that the resulting table has the required formatting. Often it will not, necessitating manual changes to the table of contents to make it conform. In a related vein, when formatting the titles of tables and the captions of figures in the body of the proposal you will have to follow specific formats specified in the dissertation template that may not be the same as the formats specified in the template for those same titles and captions in the list of tables and list of figures. Also, if you generate your lists of tables and figures automatically, you may have to revise them manually so that they conform to the standard. Finally, make sure that the page numbers for items in your table of contents and lists of tables and figures are correct. To ensure this, check them as the last step of each revision after you have made all other changes to your proposal/dissertation.

Chapter 1

In Chapter 1, you introduce your study in a way that provides an overview of its essential elements. With your IRP and the rubric in hand, you are well prepared to describe them. Table 7 shows a list of the elements generally included in Chapter 1, as well as which steps of the integrated research plan inform them.

Table 7. How the IRP informs Chapter 1

Element	**IRP Step**
Introduction/Background	All
Problem Statement	1
Theoretical Foundation	2
Purpose Statement	3
Research Questions/Hypotheses	4
Nature of the Study	5 and 6
Significance of the Study	1
Operational Definitions	6
Assumptions, Limitations, and Scope	6
Summary	All

Your university's dissertation rubric will spell out exactly what you are to cover in each of these elements of Chapter 1. Your IRP, which you developed as a coherent research plan, will provide the essential information you need to write the description of each element in a way that ensures that your overview is coherent.

You should note that the theoretical foundation is more than the grounding research study you discovered in the process of developing your IRP. It is a distillation of your literature review from Chapter 2 that indicates the area of your general field of study (e.g., management, education, psychology) you are specifically focusing on (e.g., transformational leadership, higher education, organizational psychology), and the major theories and research in that specific area that relate to your topic. You organize the overview to provide a context for the grounding literature identified in step 2 of your IRP (i.e., the specific recent work of other scholars, published in a refereed journal or a dissertation, that you will base your study on to extend the boundaries of knowledge in your field).

Operational definitions are descriptions of the meaning of words used in your dissertation, such as technical terms, that are not common knowledge, presented in the format prescribed by your university. Generally, each includes a citation which references the source of the definition. You should make up your own definitions only in those rare cases when you cannot find a suitable definition in the literature.

A colleague once described the difference between the assumptions and limitations of a study and the scope of a study in a useful way. He suggested that the former deal with the internal validity of the study (i.e., whether the study measures what you say it does), while the latter deal with the external validity of the study (i.e., whether the study results are generalizable). For example, when data collection involves interviewing or surveying study participants, the accuracy of the data (and the resulting findings from its analysis) depends on the honesty of the participants. Hence, that they will answer honestly is generally an assumption of this type of study. Similarly, if you want to know something about your participants (such as their effectiveness as leaders) that non-participants (such as their followers) can better assess, but you rely on participant (leader) self-assessments to keep the time required for data collection reasonable, you are imposing a limitation on the internal validity of your study.

Conversely, if you restrict the scope of your quantitative, survey-based study to a sample of the general population chosen from a target population of potential participants in your local area or your company because you can gain access more easily to these people, you are limiting the external validity of your study (and thus your ability to generalize the findings of your study) to the extent that this target population is not representative of the general population in which you are interested. For example, if you are interested in the general effect of servant leadership on follower satisfaction, but your sample includes only members of religious organizations to whom you have ready access as a result of your association with them, you cannot generalize your findings to leaders in nonreligious organizations.

Chapter 2

Chapter 2 contains the literature review of your proposal, which focuses on the theoretical/conceptual foundation of your study. As the term literature review suggests, in this chapter you write a topic-focused, integrated essay in which you move from a presentation of the major theories (and related current and, as necessary, classic research findings published in the refereed journals, dissertations, and other scholarly documents of your field) that are pertinent to your general topic to a more in-depth analysis, synthesis, and evaluation of particular theories and research that bear on your specific topic, leading to that singular study (or vital few studies) that is the grounding study (or studies) for your dissertation research project. In this manner, you provide a rich, coherent context for your readers to understand (to paraphrase Sir Isaac Newton) which giants' shoulders you intend to stand on.

As shown in Figure 4, one way to picture your literature review is to imagine it as a funnel. It is widest at the top (the beginning of your review) and narrowest at the bottom (the end of your review). It moves from general to specific, culminating in your grounding literature and pointing to your study. The overall effect of the review is thus to position your proposed study in the literature of your field.

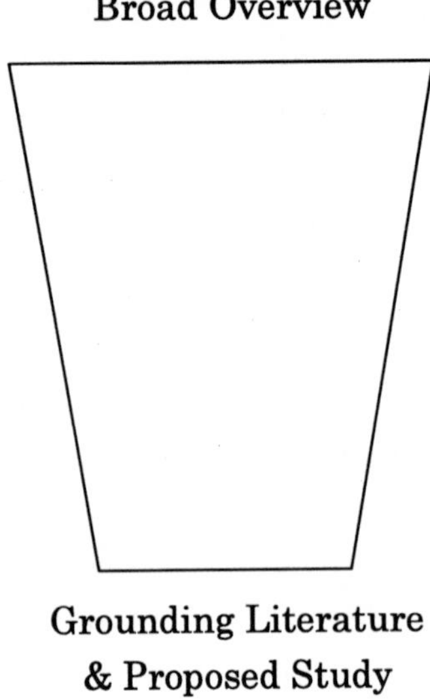

Figure 4. Literature Review as a Funnel

Another way to view your literature review is to think of it as the explanation of a series of intersecting circles, also known as a Venn diagram, where each circle represents a major theoretical aspect of your study. You start by providing a broad overview of the area outside of the circles (which is the most general), then move to an explanation of each of the circles (which are key elements of your theoretical foundation), and culminate with an in depth analysis of the intersection of each of the circles (which represents the prior work that most directly relates to your dissertation research project).

Figure 5 contains an example of a Venn diagram of the content of a hypothetical study dealing with the relationship between transformational leadership and employee motivation. The area (A) outside of the circles (i.e., which represent the domain of your study) represents the general literature on leadership, which, as the overall context for the study, you would provide a brief overview of first. One of the circles (B) represents the literature on transformational leadership, the other (C) the literature on employee motivation. You would provide more in depth and separate review of each of these areas next. Finally, the area (D) where the two circles overlap (known as the intersection) represents the literature on the relationship between the independent variable (transformational leadership) and the dependent variable (employee motivation), which you would critically analyze in the final section of the theoretical foundation section of your literature review.

[Note: I have kept these two diagrams of the structure of a literature review (i.e., Figures 4 and 5) intentionally simple to convey the underlying concepts. Your own review will undoubtedly involve a more complicated theoretical foundation, with a more elaborate (and appropriate) conceptual map of the interrelationships among the specific theories/concepts that inform your literature review, and will therefore necessitate a more elaborate structure for the review. You can learn more about conceptual mapping and writing literature reviews by reading some of the selected readings described in Part III, as well as the dissertations of other scholars in your field of study.]

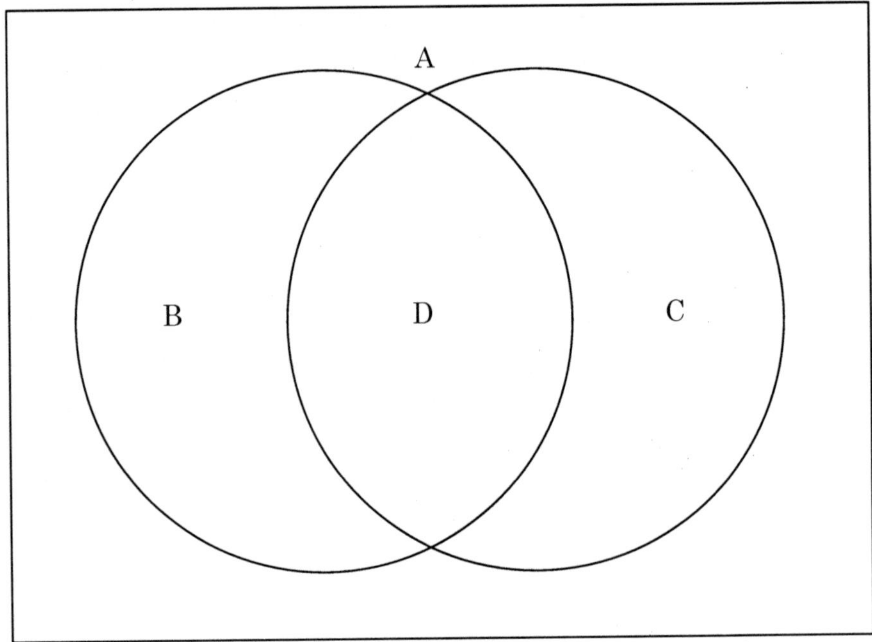

A. Leadership
B. Transformational Leadership
C. Employee Motivation
D. Transformational Leadership and Employee Motivation

Figure 5. Venn Diagram of a Hypothetical Literature Review

As with the rest of your proposal, the university's dissertation rubric and template will provide you with specific information about the required content of Chapter 2, such as the extent to which you may include classic works in your field to support the preponderance of current, topic-related literature that you must include in your literature review. In addition to reviewing the theoretical foundation of your work, you may also have to provide a review of your methodological foundation in which you identify the alternative research methods that you could use to address the problem (such as a case study, grounded theory study, or phenomenological study for a qualitative study, or a survey, experiment, or existing data analysis for a quantitative study) based on the approaches that other researchers have taken, and the reasons why you have selected a particular method (or methods) for your study. You may also have to indicate which databases your searched and what keywords you used in those searches. Regardless of what else you have to include in Chapter 2, you must present your theoretical foundation (for a quantitative study) or conceptual foundation (the equivalent for a qualitative study) in a coherent, logical, topic- and subtopic-based, critical essay that you organize carefully and write impeccably.

Chapter 3

In Chapter 3, you describe your research approach in sufficient detail for a reader to know exactly what you propose to do (and why) to collect and analyze the data you need to answer your research questions and test any hypotheses you have. Table 8 contains a typical list of the elements you must discuss in Chapter 3 of a quantitative and a qualitative and dissertation, respectively.

Table 8. Typical Elements of Chapter 3

Quantitative Proposal/ Dissertation	Qualitative Proposal/ Dissertation
✓ Introduction	✓ Introduction
✓ Research Questions & Hypotheses	✓ Research Questions & Sub Questions
✓ Justification of Research Method	✓ Justification of Research Method
✓ Population	✓ Population
✓ Sample (& Power Analysis)	✓ Sample
✓ Participant Selection Method	✓ Participant Selection Criteria
✓ Variables/Model	✓ Method of Participant Access
✓ Measurement/ Instrumentation	✓ Role of Researcher in Data Collection
✓ Data Collection and Analysis Method	✓ Data Collection and Analysis Method
✓ Ethical Safeguards	✓ Ethical Safeguards
✓ Summary	✓ Summary

It is important to note that the contents of Chapter 3 will differ depending on the type of dissertation research, quantitative or qualitative, that you are proposing to conduct. For example, as discussed in Appendix E it is important in a quantitative dissertation to know the target population and the size of the probability sample of that population you will need to select, based on a before the fact (i.e., a priori) power analysis (for a power of 80%), to have a good chance (the standard is 95%) of detecting the presence of a moderate difference (i.e., a medium effect size) between the values of the variables stipulated in your alternative and null hypotheses. In contrast, for a qualitative dissertation you will choose a target population that exhibits the characteristic you wish to study, and you will select on purpose from that target population a non-probability sample of participants of adequate size (see Appendix E) for your study. This process will result in a purposive sample, rather than the random sample required for quantitative research.

Another important difference between the research method for a quantitative versus a qualitative dissertation is the precise specification required for a quantitative study of the independent and dependent variables in your study and the model that relates them (as described in Appendix D), in comparison to a description for a qualitative study of how you will gain access to the participants you select in your purposive sample, on whose information the quality of your study rests. In each case, the issue involved is internal validity. Simply put, in this section you provide part of the answer to the following questions, respectively: Does your quantitative study measure what it purports to measure? Is your qualitative study reflective of the experiences of people who have lived the phenomenon? If you cannot find a way to measure (i.e., operationalize) your variables (or if you interview the wrong people), then you will not have valid data from which to draw valid inferences about the truth of your hypotheses (or from which to develop valid insights into the phenomenon you are studying).

[Note: Qualitative research can involve other forms of data collection than interviewing participants. Researchers often include observation of participant behavior and analysis of existing documents (e.g., written materials, videos, etc.) in qualitative research studies for the purpose of triangulation (i.e., the inclusion of several different forms of data to see if the respective analyses lead to similar or different findings). In each of these cases, however, the same principle applies; namely, if you cannot gain access to people who have lived experience of the phenomenon in which you are interested, your observations won't be reflective of your target population, and if you cannot find appropriate written material that deals specifically with the phenomenon, then analysis of it will not provide insights that pertain to the lived experiences of the target population.]

Students often use survey instruments to measure one or more of the variables in a quantitative dissertation. Whether to use an existing instrument (which is preferable if you can find one that measures one of your variables well because the developer(s) of the instrument has (have) tested it for validity and reliability using standard research measurements) or to create your own questionnaire, is a choice you will have to make. If you decide that you need to develop your own instrument, you will have to take the additional step of doing a pilot study on a small number of members of your target population to determine (a) the respondents' understanding of the questions, (b) the appropriateness of the questions, (c) the appropriateness of the length of the survey, and (d) if there are any other aspects of the study that are problematic. Based on this review, you will revise the survey as necessary. In addition, you will perform an analysis of the pilot data to test your data coding and editing procedures as well as your ability to perform the required statistical analyses.

Another important methodological issue is your role as a researcher. In a quantitative study, your role is strictly to collect data and analyze it. You are, in effect, like the scientist who does her best not to disturb the measurement process in any way so as not to invalidate the findings of the study. This search for objective truth, which is based on the traditional research paradigm of classical science (i.e. post-positivism), is one with which we are all familiar from our earlier formal schooling. Because this role is invariant across quantitative dissertations, there is no need to state it in Chapter 3. However, in qualitative research, based as it is on a newer research paradigm (i.e., constructivism) which holds that people's truth about the experiences they have lived is subjective and waiting for the researcher to discover from the participants whom he chooses to interview (or observe, or collect documents about), the interaction of the researcher with the participants in the data collection process (e.g., via interviews, and even observations) is more intrusive of necessity than in an experiment or other controlled interaction (such as the completion of a survey in private by a respondent). Hence, in Chapter 3 of a qualitative dissertation you must discuss your role in the data collection process, the effect this role may have on the quality of the data you collect (such as the potential for biasing interviewee responses, or the effect of your lack of experience in fieldwork if you are a novice at it), and how you will manage any issues that might arise based on that role.

Regardless of the nature of your dissertation—quantitative or qualitative—you will need to describe the data collection and analysis approach you intend to use in your study (addressing the elements specified in your university's dissertation rubric) in this section of Chapter 3. A data collection and analysis method used in grounded theory studies, but also often used in other types of qualitative research, is the constant comparative method. This approach differs from the two-step, sequential approach of initial data collection and subsequent data analysis used in quantitative studies in that it involves collecting and analyzing the data in parallel and interactively.

For example, you might compare the data collected from an initial interview to the data collected in a second interview to determine similarities and differences between them. Then you might compare the data collected from a third interview to the findings of the first two interviews to identify the similarities and differences among all three. This interactive process of data collection and analysis would continue until you reached a point where analysis of additional data did not alter the insights gained from (i.e., the emergent theory developed from analysis of) the previous interviews. This is the point of saturation, or redundancy. [Note: You can use the constant comparative method in the same manner to analyze data collected from observations, as well as data contained in documents.]

As you can see from Table 8, both quantitative and qualitative dissertations also require the exposition of a number of other common aspects of the research design, such as the restatement of your research questions and hypotheses (exactly as they appear in Chapter 1), a justification of your choice of research method (in comparison to other possible methods used by researchers to examine similar problems, as reported in the literature), and a review of the measures you plan to take to ensure that no harm comes to your participants as a result of participating in your study.

References

This section provides the information needed by readers to find your information sources if they wish to do so. Hence, the reference citations corresponding to all of your in-text citations belong in the list of references. Note that this is not a bibliography of resources you have use in your dissertation research. Thus, only the full citations for sources cited in your text belong in the reference list.

There should only be one list of references for your proposal (or your dissertation). You should place the word References in the center of the page above your reference citations and not bold it (because it is a title, not a heading). The list itself should follow in alphabetical order based on the last name of the primary author of the source (i.e., book, journal article, dissertation, etc.). Per APA, each reference citation should be double spaced and hanging indented by one-half inch. [Note: Some universities permit single spacing with an extra line between citations.]

Students often have trouble creating reference citations correctly (i.e., in APA style). As a result, their proposals look unprofessional and they have to revise them (based on requests for changes from reviewers) many more times than necessary to get the formatting right. To avoid these unnecessary revisions, you should learn as much about APA style as early in the proposal/dissertation writing process as possible. To that end, I suggest that you (a) carefully study the information in Appendix F, which contains a synopsis of the ABCs of APA style, (b) read and thoroughly familiarize yourself with the latest APA manual, and (c) learn about and capitalize on the resources provided by your university's writing center.

Appendices

There are many documents in a proposal/dissertation that belong in an appendix, rather than in one of the chapters, such as the consent form that the participants have to fill out to provide you with documentation of their willingness to participate in your study and your curriculum vitae. For a quantitative study, you might also include copies of your survey instrument(s), an explanation of the power analysis you used to determine the minimum sample size, summaries of the data you collected (dissertation only), pertinent details of your data analysis method and findings (dissertation only), and so forth. For a qualitative study, you might also include the list of questions you intend to ask interviewees (i.e., the interview protocol), a list of participants (coded to preserve their anonymity) and their roles, a detailed explanation of your analytical methodology (if it is not a standard one), samples of interviewee responses (dissertation only), details of various aspects of your data collection and analysis (dissertation only), and so forth.

Complete the IRB Application

While the institutional review board (IRB) application is not a formal part of the proposal, the two documents are closely related, as the proposal is one of the primary sources of information that the IRB will use to evaluate your proposed research project from an ethical perspective. The IRB's responsibility is to determine if your proposal meets the three criteria that all research projects must meet—respect for persons, beneficence, and justice (*The Belmont Report*, 1979). In addition to your proposal, the IRB will require you to submit for their review an application requesting approval to conduct your research, and any related documents they may need to make their determination.

The first of the three criteria used to evaluate your proposed research project—respect for persons—essentially requires that you give study participants the choice of whether or not to participate in your study, and that you protect those unable to make an informed choice or those whose freedom of choice is restricted, such as children or prisoners. In practice, this most often means that you must provide a consent form with a description of what you propose to do to the potential participants in your study, and that they must indicate their willingness to participate by signing the form. In the case of an online survey, taking the survey after reading the equivalent of the consent form in the introductory portion of the survey generally constitutes "informed consent."

[Note: The IRB's enforcement of this criterion often causes delays for students who wish to conduct research inside their own organization. In these cases, the issue of coercion becomes paramount to assess. If the student is in a high-level position, the IRB may see the potential for abuse as a reason for not granting permission for the study, or for requiring the implementation of special measures to ensure that people are not coerced into participating, which can result in a considerable delay in the process of gaining IRB approval. The moral of the story is that you should not plan to do research in your own organization if you have other options.]

The second criterion—beneficence—requires that your research not result in harm to any of the participants if at all possible, or that its potential benefits outweigh any harm that might occur. While this criterion is clearly applicable to medical research, where experimental protocol necessitates denying a potentially effective treatment to those in the control group for the potential long term benefit to society of knowing whether the new treatment is really more effective, it may also apply to many types of social science research. The IRB will assess whether the benefits (short or long term) outweigh the risk (of harming participants) of your proposed study. If not, the IRB may require that you modify your research design to maximize its potential benefits and minimize its potential harm before granting its approval.

Another important aspect of beneficence is ensuring the confidentiality of the participants. You do this by planning for and taking appropriate measures to disguise the identity of participants and to safeguard the data you collect from them in all phases of data collection and analysis, as well as in subsequent reporting in the dissertation and other documents (such as study reports to participating organizations, journal articles, books, and the like).

The final criterion—justice—requires that the benefits and burdens of your study be shared equally. "An injustice occurs when some benefit to which a person is entitled is denied without good reason or when some burden is imposed unduly" (*The Belmont Report*, 1979, p. 4). The IRB will determine the extent to which your proposed study meets this criterion, and, if necessary, suggest modifications to your research design.

The length of time it will take the IRB to review your application and proposal and make a decision will depend, all other things being equal, on the seriousness of the issues your proposed study raises with regard to these three criteria. As you might imagine, studies involving the use of existing data generally take the least time to review and gain approval for, while studies involving a high likelihood of harming participants if not conceived or executed properly generally take much longer. These considerations are important, but not overriding. You should design your study to obtain the best possible answers to your research questions in the most ethical manner possible, and let the IRB help you to make it even better.

Chapter 6

Conducting the Research

After working so hard to gain approval to conduct your research, getting the go ahead from IRB can be like a shot of adrenalin. You are finally free to send out that survey (or an email invitation to participate if it is an online survey), to interview that first participant, or to otherwise begin your data collection. Following the steps you laid out in your proposal based on your IRP, and with your methodology manual(s) firmly in hand, you will collect and analyze your data (if your research is quantitative in nature), or you will collect and then analyze your initial data, then collect more data, analyze it, and compare your findings to the initial data results (using the constant comparative method) in an ongoing process of developing insight into a phenomenon (if your research is qualitative in nature). [Note: You will find more information on books that are acceptable for use as guides to dissertation research methodology (i.e., methodology manuals in my terminology) in the Selected Readings section of Part III.]

Along the way, you will deal with a number of real world issues, such as insufficient participation (fewer than the minimum sample size) or incomplete data in a quantitative study, or unavailable (due to travel, job changes, etc.) or uncooperative participants in a qualitative study. To surmount each of these obstacles, you will work closely with your committee members, particularly your chair and methodologist, and outside resources, such as a statistician if you choose to incur the extra expense of employing one to help you (and, of course, if and only if your university permits it) and other appropriate experts.

If your dissertation is quantitative, you will need to analyze your data using statistical software to test your hypotheses. This may impose some real challenges if statistics is not your strong point. But even if it is, be prepared for your methodologist to review the findings of your data analyses in detail to ensure that you have performed the analysis properly. In my experience, only a small percentage of students are able to do this. So, you should expect to have to run your numbers several times, initially on your own, and later to correct mistakes identified by your methodologist (or statistician if you have one). It is important to note that data analysis is not the only area that can prove problematic. You must edit your data carefully before you analyze it to eliminate (or otherwise deal with) instances of missing or erroneous data. Then you must carefully follow the protocol of your statistical software package when entering your data sets. For example, if you are performing a simple regression analysis, you must enter the data sets for your independent and dependent variables in the proper column (as indicated by your software). If not, you will obtain a perfectly valid looking analysis that is nonetheless meaningless.

As you can see, just plugging numbers you have collected into a statistical package and presenting the results in your dissertation is not enough. To ensure that those results make statistical sense, (a) you must edit your data carefully first. Then (b) you must enter your data into the right statistical routine (c) in the correct places to obtain meaningful results. Based on certain information included in the statistical analysis provided by your software, (d) you must then check to see if your data violate the assumptions underlying the statistical test(s) you are using. If they satisfy those assumptions, then (e) you are finally in a position to use the output from your statistical software package to test your hypotheses.

In a qualitative dissertation, you face a different set of challenges. Because the researcher is the primary data collection instrument in studies that rely on interviews or observations, issues of researcher bias, skill at interviewing or observing, facility with the data collection and analysis method (like constant comparative analysis), ability to write a qualitative report that reflects the insights gleaned from the data without presenting it all, among others make your task in many ways as daunting as collecting and analyzing statistical data properly is to a student doing quantitative research.

Despite the many challenges of this phase of the research process, it is a very exciting time during which you experience the thrill of discovery that comes from performing a scientifically sound investigation into the nature of an important issue in your professional field; one on which, by dint of all of your hard work, you have become a leading authority. Like a great detective, you attempt to solve the mystery and thereby provide answers to the important questions that guide your research into a problem of social significance.

Chapter 7

Writing the Dissertation

As shown previously in Table 6, the dissertation is basically the proposal with the addition of two chapters. In Chapter 4, you describe the findings of your study. In Chapter 5, you interpret your findings and make recommendations for their practical application and for future research. While your university's dissertation rubric will be specify exactly what you are to cover in Chapters 4 and 5, the following are some of the elements that appear in most dissertations.

Chapter 4

Begin Chapter 4 by briefly reviewing the purpose of your study and providing an overview of the chapter. Organize the chapter around your research questions/hypotheses, presenting each one, and your findings about it, separately. For a quantitative study, present the descriptive statistics for your sample first; then provide the results of each hypothesis test based on the data you collected from those participants; and, if necessary, identify and discuss any issues (such as violations of the assumptions underlying your statistical tests) that you discovered when analyzing your data and how you dealt with them. Conclude with a summary of your findings. Your goal in writing this chapter is to present enough information (in the text and related appendices) so that people reading your dissertation can understand what you learned about your hypotheses based on your statistical analyses, and can judge the extent to which your findings are valid and generalizable.

For a qualitative study, focus on describing the process you followed and what you learned as a result of applying your qualitative data collection and analysis method, such as the constant comparative method. Explain the characteristics of your sample and examine any issues that arose and how you dealt with them. In particular, describe the procedures you followed to ensure the quality of your data (e.g., member checks, peer examination, use of data tracking systems, and triangulation). Conclude with a summary of your findings relative to your research questions. Again, your goal is to satisfy the needs of a reader about what you did and what you found in a way that supports the validity and credibility of your results.

When writing Chapter 4, it is important to present your findings according to the principle that *more is less*. That is, focus on providing a sufficient amount of information to explain what you discovered, but no more. For example, in a quantitative dissertation provide important statistics, such as correlation coefficients, *t*-scores, *F*-scores, and the like (in APA style) in the text (or in tables if there are many statistics), and briefly summarize your interpretation of those key statistics in the text. Do not present output documents from your statistical package (either in the text or an appendix), as that would be redundant. Likewise, do not describe in the text exactly the same information that is in your tables. Instead, describe only the most important points. Also, do not present scatter plots or other statistical diagrams in the text. Describe their implications in the text but place them in appendices, and then only if they are necessary to support your findings. In a qualitative dissertation, provide examples of data (from transcripts, memos, journals, and the like) to support your assertions about the themes, relationships, and theory that emerged from your study, but do not describe or make available all of your data. In summary, when writing Chapter 4, keep your writing precise and succinct, like a journalist reporting the facts about what you learned from your study in a clear and credible manner.

Chapter 5

In Chapter 5, (a) draw conclusions about the meaning of your findings (relative to your research questions) in light of the existing literature and the objectives of your study, (b) discuss the implications of your results and make suggestions for the practical application of your findings, and (c) make recommendations for future study. If necessary, discuss any potential limitations of your findings, such as any that might have resulted from your personal biases (in a qualitative study) or any measurement or statistical anomalies (in a quantitative study), before drawing conclusions or making recommendations for future action or research. Conclude Chapter 5 with a brief summary your findings and a clear statement of the potential impact of your research.

Chapter 8

Publishing the Findings

Although publishing the results of your dissertation is generally not a requirement for earning a doctorate, it is something that you should seriously consider doing after you complete your dissertation. This not only adds to the body of knowledge contained in the formally published literature in your field (which is something that is important to do), it also provides you with the motivation to continue to do research. While publication will be an imperative if you choose an academic career, it is not required in most other professions. Hence, getting some part of your dissertation research published can play a vital role in instilling in you the desire to conduct further research (on your own) when the need to do research (under the tutelage of others) to earn a terminal degree (a doctorate) no longer exists.

While there are many potential outlets for your work (e.g., a book, a chapter in edited collection, a magazine article), the most typical is the refereed journal. Hence, publishing in an established, peer-reviewed journal should be your primary goal. Although there are many ways of becoming a published author, here is some advice that my students have found useful.

✓ First, identify several journals that are possible publishers for your work. As a doctoral student, you have read many refereed journal articles; hence, you should be familiar with some of the important journals in your field. The reference lists of articles particularly relevant to your dissertation topic (such as those you used in your literature review) should provide other ideas to add to your list of potential journals.

- ✓ Second, go to the website of each journal and learn about the types of articles they publish.
- ✓ Third, if you think that your article might be of interest to the editors of a particular journal, read the author submission guidelines to see if you can comply with them.
- ✓ Fourth, if you feel confident that you can prepare a manuscript that meets their needs, print out or store the guidelines for use in preparing your article.
- ✓ Fifth, read several articles published in the journal carefully to get a feel for their content, structure, and formatting.
- ✓ Sixth, prepare and submit a manuscript in APA style but tailored to meet the *exact* specifications of the journal.
- ✓ Seventh, work collaboratively with the editor and peer reviewer(s) to revise your manuscript until they deem it to be acceptable for publication.
- ✓ Eighth, if they do not accept your submission, do not become discouraged. Simply submit your manuscript, revised if you think it will be stronger based on the feedback you received from the peer reviewers, to another journal. Continue to do so until a journal publishes your article.
- ✓ Finally, celebrate your success, and, if you haven't already done so, start doing the research for your next article.

Before concluding this section, I want to elaborate on step six, which is to prepare and submit a manuscript that meets the *exact* specifications of the publication, because it is so important to the process of getting an article published. While there are many "rookie mistakes" that you can make that hurt your chances of convincing a journal editor to publish your article, one that definitely brands you as an amateur is submitting a document that does not meet the author guidelines of the publication (such as submitting your dissertation in its original form). If the guidelines instruct you to submit a manuscript of up to a certain length, but no longer, make sure that your submission satisfies the requirement. If the guidelines specify that you write in the first person, then do so. If they indicate that you should follow the latest APA style guidelines, do it. Think of it this way. If you want to maximize the chances of your article appearing in that journal, do everything necessary to prepare a manuscript that looks professional to the editor(s)—that is, which adheres to their specified submission guidelines precisely.

Write your original manuscript in accordance with the form and style guidelines in the APA's publication manual (American Psychological Association, 2010), which expertly describes the process of manuscript creation. Modify it subject to the requirements contained in the journal's author submission guidelines (as discussed in the previous paragraph). For example, revise the headings, in-text citations, and reference citations in your manuscript so that they are in the *exact* format required by the journal if the journal does not use APA style headings or citations. This approach should ensure that your manuscript looks professional to the editor and peer reviewer(s), who can then judge it solely on the merit of its content (which is all that you or any other author can ask for), rather than being influenced by any obvious shortcomings in its form and style.

Conclusion

With what you have learned so far about dissertation research (in Part I) and dissertation writing (in Part II), you have the necessary knowledge to craft an excellent dissertation. One that (a) demonstrates convincingly to your university that you have the ability to design, conduct, and report the findings of a research project—thus earning you the coveted doctorate, and that (b) makes an important contribution to the literature of your field. In Part III, you will discover other resources, such as (a) advice on how to choose a dissertation committee and (b) how to manage the dissertation process, as well as (c) suggestions for further reading and (d) supplementary information in the appendices that can help you to enhance various parts of your proposal/dissertation as well as accelerate your progress towards its completion.

Part III

Dissertation Resources

Chapter 9

Enabling the Dissertation Process

Earning a doctorate is not just about writing a quality dissertation. That is necessary, but not sufficient. Besides selecting a dissertation committee whose members have the expertise to assist you in crafting your dissertation, you must choose a chair with the knowledge and competence to guide you through the dissertation review process. Because choosing the members of your dissertation committee is a crucial decision that can make the difference between earning a doctorate or being ABD, you need to do so with care. But how do you decide who should be on your committee and why they should be on it?

Choosing a Committee

Committee selection starts on the first day of your program. Take advantage of every opportunity you have to meet the faculty in your area of interest, especially if you are pursuing your doctorate via a distance education program and will not see the faculty on a regular basis like students in a bricks and mortar institution, to determine which of them you might want on your dissertation committee when the time comes. Some of the decision criteria you should consider in selecting committee members are:

- ✓ Expertise
- ✓ Chemistry
- ✓ Responsiveness
- ✓ Student Centeredness
- ✓ Interest and Availability

Expertise

You want faculty on your committee who have content and methodological expertise. A content person will help you to (a) ground your research in the literature, (b) design a research project that has the potential to add new knowledge to your field of study, and (c) interpret the meaning of your findings in relation to the existing literature in your field. A methodology expert will help you to design and conduct a research project to answer your research questions (or test your hypotheses) in a way that follows accepted research methods, and thus has internal validity, reliability, and external validity. [Note: Although the individuals on your committee should collectively provide you with both sets of expertise, this does not necessarily mean that you need a content expert *and* a methods expert. One person may provide both types of expertise.]

Chemistry

Other than the obvious need to find faculty with the expertise you require to complete your dissertation successfully, it is imperative that you relate and work well with the people on your committee. Because completing a dissertation is a time consuming and demanding activity, it is better to think of your committee, especially your chair, as potential colleagues rather than as mere advisors. If you find a highly qualified faculty member who could provide needed expertise, but to whom you do not relate well, do not ask that person to serve on your dissertation committee. Life is just too short to put up with the aggravation that might come from trying to work with such a person.

Ideally, you will want to construct a harmonious committee. Your dissertation chair can really help you to find the right people with the right chemistry. After all, he or she will be the primary guide on your doctoral journey. So, put together a preliminary list of candidates using these five criteria and others of your own, but expect your chair to have a major say, if not the final say, about which of these faculty members, or others you may not have considered, would work well together and provide the necessary expertise.

Responsiveness

While expertise, and to a lesser extent chemistry, are characteristics that occur to most students when considering potential dissertation committee members, responsiveness is one that many fail to consider. It is incumbent on you to assess the responsiveness of each potential committee member. There are many ways to do this, including (a) working with the person, (b) talking with other students who have worked with or had the individual as an instructor or mentor, (c) sending an email or leaving a voice mail message to test the person's responsiveness unobtrusively, or (d) just asking the individual about his or her policy on responding to students. Use any method you wish, but do not fail to determine the responsiveness of each potential member of your committee. Otherwise, when your patience is at its ebb from waiting for what seems like an interminable time for a response to a question or a review of a proposal or dissertation draft, you will regret your lack of diligence.

Student Centeredness

One of the most important criteria that you should consider when selecting committee members is whether or not they are student centered. By student centered I mean that they are truly concerned about their students' well-being, and will do what it takes to enable them to learn and succeed. Given the unique demands of the dissertation, which is a new learning experience for all who undertake it as well as a demonstration of research competence by a student whose research skills are in the early stages of development, the importance of having student-centered committee members who are patient and supportive can hardly be overstated. Personal experience and reputation are the two best ways to assess the student centeredness of potential dissertation committee members.

Interest and Availability

Once you have made your selections, you can ask each of the faculty on your list if they would be willing to serve on your committee. Each request should include an overview or prospectus summarizing your proposed dissertation so that the faculty member can see what you are asking him or her to sign on for.

Your committee members are people, not just distinguished academicians. Keeping this in mind will help you to deal with them in a manner that satisfies your objectives and meets their needs. Be respectful of faculty commitments and don't take offense if some of them are not interested in your particular proposed study or are not available to serve on your committee. In that case, just move on to other faculty on your list and keep asking until you have assembled your team.

The Chair

The chair plays a crucial role on your committee. This individual, more than any other, will affect the time it takes to complete your dissertation, as well as the quality of your experience during the process. Ideally, your chair will have all five of the characteristics described above—expertise, chemistry, responsiveness, student centeredness, and interest/availability—

and will have a clear understanding of the steps in the dissertation review process at your institution. In addition, an ideal chair will be savvy about the informal aspects of the dissertation review process, such as who to contact for clarification of a requirement or resolution of a problem, as well as when and how to do so most effectively. Faculty members who have been associated with an institution for some time typically have this type of insight into its inner workings. Finally, the ideal chair will be someone respected by other faculty and students who has a track record of helping students to complete their dissertations and graduate in a timely manner.

Managing the Process

Who is in charge of your dissertation review process, you, your dissertation chair, or other committee members? Simply put, you must take charge of the process and work collaboratively with your chair. After all, you are the one who wants to complete the dissertation and receive your doctorate. However, this does not mean that you control the efforts of your committee directly. Your dissertation chair must play the role of facilitator on your committee.

For example, you and the chair will work on your dissertation proposal together. When the chair says it is ready, he or she will then either send your proposal to the other members of the committee on your behalf or direct you to do so. From that point, you will interact with the committee when and only as directed by your chair until the process is completed. While you retain the responsibility for submitting certain required documents to your university (such as the IRB application), your chair is responsible for submitting your proposal, dissertation, and supporting documents to university reviewers on your behalf at various stages of the review process.

Conflict Resolution

Another aspect of your chair's role as facilitator involves the resolution of conflicts between committee members. Imagine that, despite your best efforts, things get out of control at some point in the review process. Say, for instance, that two members of your committee disagree on what each considers an important aspect of your dissertation. To satisfy one, you must displease the other. What do you do?

Whether your university bases its dissertation review process on a consensus model or not, I suggest that you immediately involve your dissertation chair in a conflict resolution process designed to get all of the members of your committee, including the two who are at odds, to agree on what you need to change and how. If you do not do this, but instead make unilateral changes in response to either member's requests, you will find yourself revising constantly and still never completely satisfying your committee.

Remember that consensus does not mean unanimous agreement. Consensus means that everyone either agrees on what you have to do or is neutral but can live with the group's decision. This important outcome is, surprisingly, not as difficult to achieve as some people believe, especially when the participants engage in a collaborative process of discussing the problem and determining a solution. A telephone conference, convened and facilitated by your chair at your request, is a very good method for arriving at a consensus decision about a knotty problem because it engages you (if appropriate) and all of your committee members simultaneously in the conflict resolution.

Oral Defense

Your chair is also the facilitator for the oral defense of your proposal (if your university requires one) and your dissertation. As such, your chair must prepare you for the expectations set by the university for an oral defense, including the nature of the presentation you will have to make, the type of questions you can expect participants to ask, how to handle difficult situations that may arise, and any other aspects of the oral that your chair feels you need to know about in advance.

Bumps in the Road

The gentleman who was president of the university when I started my doctoral journey gave a group of students assembled at a doctoral residency some very sage advice that went something like this: "If you want to achieve your goal of earning a Ph.D., then you need to treat every unexpected thing that happens along the way as a bump in the road." What he meant was that if you treat as a crisis each problem that occurs while you are pursuing your doctorate, such as an issue with the bursar related to your student loan, a misunderstanding with a professor, or even a life situation that arises, you will expend energy unnecessarily and possibility lose the momentum you have built that is enabling you to move toward your goal.

Realizing the inherent wisdom in this approach, I treated every unexpected event that happened to me in the course of my doctoral program as a bump in the road. In practice, this meant that I had to handle gracefully and to the best of my ability each situation that threatened to derail me from the pursuit of the doctorate, but that I would not let that situation, no matter how serious, prevent me from continuing my doctoral studies. This approach enabled me to deal effectively with a number of minor and major challenges I unexpectedly faced on my unique doctoral journey and, as a result, to earn my Ph.D. in the minimum time allowed by my university. I urge you to consider adopting "bumps in the road" as your motto. It will be very helpful to you in managing the vagaries of the dissertation review process.

Chapter 10

Selected Readings

As you have no doubt realized, one of the basic principles influencing the structure and content of this book is KISS (Keep It Simple and Sincere). Too many books on the subject of research provide so much detail in such stilted academic language that students fail to grasp the essence of dissertation research and the dissertation review process. For example, most books on research leave out the crucial initial step of creating an integrated research plan, or they just mention it in passing. Yet it is at the initial stage of the dissertation, when students know the least about the review process, that they must identify a topic that they will work on for the several years it will take to complete the dissertation. And it is precisely at this stage that most doctoral students falter and invariably end up wasting a lot of time making needless revisions to a proposal based on an unworkable (i.e., not researchable) or barely workable topic. The act of developing an integrated research plan (IRP), by following the steps described in Part I of the book, is exactly what students need to do at this critical early point in the process to minimize unnecessary revisions and thus accelerate their progress.

In this chapter, you will find brief annotations for suggested resources selected from a myriad of possible choices because (a) they are particularly relevant to your effort to complete your doctorate by designing, conducting, and reporting the findings of an exemplary dissertation (providing you with additional information that will facilitate your task), and (b) I have found them helpful and, therefore, used them either as a doctoral student anxious to produce a high quality dissertation in the shortest possible time (to keep the cost of the coveted Ph.D. reasonable), or now as a teacher of research methods at the doctoral level and as a dissertation committee chair and methodologist to help my students and mentees achieve their goals. I have organized the descriptions of these additional resources into five categories—dissertation guides, general resources, qualitative research, quantitative research, and mixed methods research.

Dissertation Guides

Surviving Your Dissertation

Rudenstam, K. E., & Newton, R. R. (2007). *Surviving your dissertation: A comprehensive guide to content and process* (3rd ed.). Thousand Oaks, CA: Sage.

Dissertation & Scholarly Research

Simon, M. K. (2006). *Dissertation & scholarly research: Recipes for success.* Dubuque, IA: Kendall/Hunt.

I used earlier editions of each of these two books when I was a doctoral student and found both of them to be helpful. Each contains detailed information on dissertation research written in a readable style that you can use to supplement what you have learned in this book if you so desire.

General Resources

Pocket Guide to APA Style

Perrin, R. (2009). *Pocket guide to APA style* (3rd ed.). Boston, MA: Wadsworth.

Before the American Psychological Association (APA) published its latest publication manual (American Psychological Association, 2010), finding the correct way to cite a source by searching the APA manual was always a challenge. This book made the process much simpler, and the most recent edition based on the latest APA manual still does. Imagine examples of the most frequently used citations (in-text and reference) for books, articles, electronic sources, and the like in one convenient, small, spiral-bound paperback book that you can open and lay flat on your desk whenever you need it, and you will understand why I find this book to be so very helpful.

Literature Reviews Made Easy

Dawidowicz, P. (2009). *Literature reviews made easy: A quick guide to success*. Bloomington, IN: ISES Press.

The best resource I have read on the subject, this book will show you how to write an excellent literature review (i.e., Chapter 2 of your dissertation). You will learn how to identify and include relevant literature in your review and present it in a way that demonstrates higher order critical thinking (i.e., analysis, synthesis, and evaluation).

Practical Statistics

Levasseur, R. E. (2006). *Practical statistics*. Annapolis, MD: MindFire Press.

If you are math phobic and thus concerned about how you will understand and defend the statistics in your quantitative dissertation, then this book is for you. After an exhaustive review of so-called "basic" books on the subject with the intention of finding one that I could recommend to my students, I found them to be anything but basic. So I decided to write a book that anyone who wants to learn about statistics for work, school, research, or the sheer enjoyment of gaining new knowledge could read. This book takes you step-by-step through the fundamental concepts of descriptive statistics, like average and standard deviation, to more advanced material on inferential methods, such as sampling theory (the basis of hypothesis testing, which every quantitative dissertation entails) and multiple regression analysis.

Student to Scholar

Levasseur, R. E. (2006). *Student to scholar: The guide for doctoral students.* Annapolis, MD: MindFire Press.

If you are currently working on about to start working on your dissertation, then you do not need this book. However, if you are just starting your doctoral journey, this book is for you. My goal in writing a book like this, which I searched for but did not find when I was a doctoral student, was to share my experiences about what it takes to get the most out of the time, money, and effort you invest in your doctoral program. As I had completed my degree in the minimum amount of time allowed and been hired by my university to work as a full-time faculty member, I felt qualified to do so. From *Student to Scholar* you will learn what it means to be a scholar, four keys to accelerate your doctoral program, how to write a major scholarly paper, how to write an annotation of a journal article, and much more.

Qualitative Research

Qualitative Research: A Guide

Merriam, S. B. (2009). *Qualitative research: A guide to design and implementation* (Rev. ed.). San Francisco, CA: Jossey-Bass.

This book provides an excellent introduction to qualitative research methods. I highly recommend it as the first book to read on the subject. It will greatly facilitate your understanding of the more in-depth methodology manual that you will need to follow in doing your dissertation research, such as Yin (2003) or Stake (1995) for case study; Glaser and Strauss (1967/2009), Corbin and Strauss (2008), or Charmaz (2006) for grounded theory; Moustakas (1994) for phenomenology; Clandinin and Connelly (2000) for narrative inquiry; and so on. [Note: There are many excellent methodology manuals in each area of research. Unless you are like me and want to assemble a library of related reference works in your field of specialization, you should ask your chair for a recommendation before purchasing one of them.]

Qualitative Research Design

Maxwell, J. A. (2005). *Qualitative research design: An iterative approach* (2nd ed.). Thousand Oaks, CA: Sage.

I like the way this author thinks and writes. He is more analytical than most in writing about the general subject of qualitative research design, and he writes in a very straightforward, readable style. In that sense, his book complements this one. If you are similarly inclined (i.e., an analytical thinker with a preference for good, clear writing), I highly recommend Maxwell's book. [Note: The section on dealing with threats to the validity of a qualitative study alone is worth the price of the book, but it contains much more of value.]

Case Study Research

Yin, R. K. (2003). *Case study research: Design and methods* (3rd ed.). Thousand Oaks, CA: Sage.

Another analytical thinker who writes in a clear, readable style, Yin is a strong advocate for the wide range of applicability of case studies, from exploration (the traditional domain of qualitative research) to explanation (the traditional domain of quantitative research). This is my favorite book on case study methodology for the same reasons that I like Maxwell's (2005) book on qualitative research design.

The Art of Case Study Research

Stake, R. E. (1995). *The art of case study research.* Thousand Oaks, CA: Sage.

Whereas Yin describes case study methodology at an abstract, conceptual level and in an analytical way, Stake focuses more on the how to do a case study using practical examples to illustrate the craft of case study research. Like Yin (2003), this is an excellent methodological guide for doing case study research.

The Discovery of Grounded Theory

Glaser, B. G., & Strauss, A. L. (1967/2009). *The discovery of grounded theory: Strategies for qualitative research.* New Brunswick, NJ: Aldine Transaction.

As the title suggests, this book tells the story of how and why the authors created the grounded theory methodology. If you choose to do a qualitative dissertation using grounded theory as your approach, then you owe it to yourself to read this book first.

Basics of Qualitative Research (Grounded Theory)

Corbin, J., & Strauss, A. (2008). *Basics of qualitative research: Techniques and procedures for developing grounded theory* (3rd ed.). Thousand Oaks, CA: Sage.

Corbin was a disciple of Strauss, one of the originators of grounded theory. This book is highly readable and presents the essentials of grounded theory in a straightforward manner. I recommend this book to all of my dissertation students who are analytical in nature and want to build a grounded theory to explain a phenomenon.

Constructing Grounded Theory

Charmaz, K. (2006). *Constructing grounded theory: A practical guide through qualitative analysis.* Thousand Oaks, CA: Sage.

In this excellent, step-by-step guide, Charmaz presents a variation on the grounded theory approach developed by Glaser and Strauss (2008) that many students, particularly those who are drawn to the constructivist world view, appreciate. It is easy to understand and full of specific examples of the elements of grounded theory development, such as memo writing, coding, and writing a literature review.

Phenomenological Research Methods

Moustakas, C. (1994). *Phenomenological research methods.* Thousand Oaks, CA: Sage.

This is a step-by-step guide for conducting a phenomenological study. It contains both a concise description of the methodology and examples of how to apply it.

Narrative Inquiry

Clandinin, D. J., & Connelly, F. M. (2000). *Narrative inquiry: Experience and story in qualitative research.* San Francisco, CA: Jossey-Bass.

Recommended to me by a colleague who used it to craft an award winning dissertation based on his one-on-one meetings with a small number of senior managers who shared a common experience (in which they told their respective stories of what happened), this book contains a clear description, augmented by numerous illustrative examples, of the steps involved in understanding people's lived experiences by means of narrative inquiry.

Qualitative Data Analysis

Miles, M. B., & Huberman, A. M. (1994). *Qualitative data analysis* (2nd ed.). Thousand Oaks, CA: Sage.

This is not a methodology manual. It is, as the title suggests, a compendium of numerous models, frameworks, diagrams, and other tools useful to qualitative researchers who seek to make meaning of their qualitative data. For example, you will find an excellent description of how to build a theoretical framework (i.e., conceptual map) in this reference.

Quantitative Research

Experimental and Quasi-Experimental Designs

Campbell, D. T., & Stanley, J. C. (1963). *Experimental and quasi-experimental designs for research.* USA: Rand McNally.

A classic in the field, this book contains examples of experimental designs, and a variety of non-experimental designs, along with an in-depth discussion of the threats to the internal and external validity of each.

Survey Research Methods

Babbie, E. (1998). *Survey research methods* (2nd ed.). Belmont, CA: Wadsworth.

Fowler, F. J. (2009). *Survey research methods* (4th ed.). Thousand Oaks, CA: Sage.

Each of these books is excellent in its own right. Babbie's is a classic work on the subject; while Fowler's is a more modern treatment, which contains a good discussion of survey data collection methods (including the use of the Internet), that many of my students doing survey research use.

Practical Meta-Analysis

Lipsey, M. W., & Wilson, D. B. (2001). *Practical meta-analysis.* Thousand Oaks, CA: Sage.

There are many methodology manuals that you might choose to guide you through the steps of a meta-analysis. However, I reviewed this one when I was preparing to do my dissertation, and selected it because it was highly readable, very precise about what to do and why to do it, and the most up-to-date manual available at the time. I highly recommend it if you have the interest and strong statistical background required to perform an analysis of the existing primary empirical research on your topic.

Mixed Methods Research

Mixed Methodology

Tashakori, A., & Teddlie, C. (1998). *Mixed methodology: Combining qualitative and quantitative approaches.* Thousand Oaks, CA: Sage.

In this book, the authors explain the difference between quantitative, qualitative, and mixed methods studies, present methods and strategies for mixed methods research, and provide examples and applications of mixed methods research from published and unpublished sources.

Foundations of Mixed Methods Research

Teddlie, C., & Tashakori, A. (2009). *Foundations of mixed methods research: Integrating quantitative and qualitative approaches in the social and behavioral sciences.* Thousand Oaks, CA: Sage.

In this book, the authors update their previous work on the subject, providing both a historical perspective on the evolution of mixed methods research as a distinct paradigm (rather than an approach that consists of a simple combination of a quantitative and a qualitative study in one research project), and a description of the methods and strategies that best suit mixed methods research. This is an excellent resource with many examples and other worthwhile features, which I highly recommend if conducting a high quality dissertation study of your topic dictates that you use a mixed methods approach.

Conclusion

This chapter consisted of brief annotations of several research-related books that my doctoral students engaged in dissertation research and I have found useful. Unless directed to do so by you chair, you need not buy any of them to achieve your goal of earning a doctoral degree. But applying the ideas in some of them might make your task a little easier or less time consuming and improve the quality of your dissertation.

References

American Psychological Association. (2010). *Publication manual of the American Psychological Association* (6th ed.). Washington, DC: Author.

Babbie, E. (1998). *Survey research methods* (2nd ed.). Belmont, CA: Wadsworth.

Barling, J., Fullugar, C., & Kelloway, E. K. (1992). *The union and its members: A psychological approach.* New York, NY: Oxford University Press.

Barling, J., Weber, T., & Kelloway, E. K. (1996). Effects of transformational leadership training on attitudinal and financial outcomes: A field experiment. *Journal of Applied Psychology, 81*(6), 827–832. doi:10.1037/0021-9010.81.6.827

Bezzebutz, J. (2009). *Creating sustainable organizational change: A grounded theory approach* (Doctoral dissertation). Available from ProQuest Dissertations and Theses database. (UMI No. 3379791)

Bloom, B. S. (Ed.). (1956/1969). *Taxonomy of educational objectives: The classification of educational goals.* New York, NY: David McKay.

Campbell, D. T., & Stanley, J. C. (1963). *Experimental and quasi-experimental designs for research.* USA: Rand McNally.

Charmaz, K. (2006). *Constructing grounded theory: A practical guide through qualitative analysis.* Thousand Oaks, CA: Sage.

Clandinin, D. J., & Connelly, F. M. (2000). *Narrative inquiry: Experience and story in qualitative research.* San Francisco, CA: Jossey-Bass.

Conger, J. A., & Kanungo, R. N. (1987). Toward a behavioral theory of charismatic leadership in organizational settings. *Academy of Management Review, 12*, 637–647. doi:10.2307/258069

Corbin, J., & Strauss, A. (2008). *Basics of qualitative research: Techniques and procedures for developing grounded theory* (3rd ed.). Thousand Oaks, CA: Sage.

Dawidowicz, P. (2009). *Literature reviews made easy: A quick guide to success.* Bloomington, IN: ISES Press.

DeGroot, T., Kiker, D. S., & Cross, T. C. (2000). A meta-analysis to review organizational outcomes related to charismatic leadership. *Canadian Journal of Administrative Sciences, 17*(4), 356–371. Retrieved from http://cjas.mcmaster.ca/index_e.htm

Drucker, P. F. (1995, February). Really inventing government. *Atlantic Monthly, 275*(2), 49–52, 54, 56, 57, 60, 61. Retrieved from http://www.theatlantic.com/

Fowler, F. J. (2009). *Survey research methods* (4th ed.). Thousand Oaks, CA: Sage.

Franklin, S. D. (2010). *The influence of spirituality on servant leadership among small business entrepreneurs* (Doctoral dissertation). Available from ProQuest Dissertations and Theses database. (UMI No. 3427302)

Glaser, B. G., & Strauss, A. L. (1967/2009). *The discovery of grounded theory: Strategies for qualitative research.* New Brunswick, NJ: Aldine Transaction.

Gouker, T. (2009). *Information technology-enabled change management: An investigation of individual experiences* (Doctoral dissertation). Available from ProQuest Dissertations and Theses database. (UMI No. 3369701)

Greenburg, D. S. (2010). *Assessing the effects of transshipments on profit in a two-echelon supply chain* (Doctoral dissertation). Available from ProQuest Dissertations and Theses database. (UMI No. 3424332)

Johnson, D. W., & Johnson, R. T. (1989). *Cooperation and competition: Theory and research.* Edina, MN: Interaction Book Company.

Levasseur, R. E. (2004). *The impact of a transforming leadership style on follower performance and satisfaction: A meta-analysis* (Doctoral dissertation). Available from ProQuest Dissertations and Theses database. (UMI No. 3138846)

Levasseur, R. E. (2005). People skills: Change management tools—leading teams. *Interfaces, 35*(2), 179–180. doi:10.1287/inte.1050.0132

Levasseur, R. E. (2006). *Practical statistics.* Annapolis, MD: MindFire Press.

Levasseur, R. E. (2006). *Student to scholar: The guide for doctoral students.* Annapolis, MD: MindFire Press.

Lipsey, M. W., & Wilson, D. B. (2001). *Practical meta-analysis.* Thousand Oaks, CA: Sage.

Maxwell, J. A. (2005). *Qualitative research design: An iterative approach* (2nd ed.). Thousand Oaks, CA: Sage.

Merriam, S. B. (2009). *Qualitative research: A guide to design and implementation* (Rev. ed.). San Francisco, CA: Jossey-Bass.

Miles, M. B., & Huberman, A. M. (1994). *Qualitative data analysis* (2nd ed.). Thousand Oaks, CA: Sage.

Moustakas, C. (1994). *Phenomenological research methods.* Thousand Oaks, CA: Sage.

Perrin, R. (2009). *Pocket guide to APA style* (3rd ed.). Boston, MA: Wadsworth.

Rudenstam, K. E., & Newton, R. R. (2007). *Surviving your dissertation: A comprehensive guide to content and process* (3rd ed.). Thousand Oaks, CA: Sage.

Schilling, L. M. (2010). *A historical analysis of the relationship between charisma and the making of great leaders* (Doctoral dissertation). Available from ProQuest Dissertations and Theses database. (UMI No. 3397897)

Simon, M. K. (2006). *Dissertation & scholarly research: Recipes for success.* Dubuque, IA: Kendall/Hunt.

Stake, R. E. (1995). *The art of case study research.* Thousand Oaks, CA: Sage.

Strunk, W., & White, E. B. (1979). *The elements of style* (3rd ed.). USA: Macmillan.

Tashakori, A., & Teddlie, C. (1998). *Mixed methodology: Combining qualitative and quantitative approaches.* Thousand Oaks, CA: Sage.

Teddlie, C., & Tashakori, A. (2009). *Foundations of mixed methods research: Integrating quantitative and qualitative approaches in the social and behavioral sciences.* Thousand Oaks, CA: Sage.

The Belmont Report. (1979). Retrieved from http://cms.umaryland.edu/bin/q/l/BelmontReport.pdf

Yin, R. K. (2003). *Case study research: Design and methods* (3rd ed.). Thousand Oaks, CA: Sage.

Appendix A

Searching Online Databases

There are many ways to search an online database for published articles. I learned the following method from the head librarian at my university, and have used it to help students quickly and effectively ground their dissertation research ideas in the literature. In concert with the technique I will describe for identifying the keywords that represent your study, it provides a powerful lens through which to view the existing work in any potential area of research. Used properly, it can lead you to one of those most desirable (Eureka!) moments when you are searching for a researchable dissertation topic.

The Method

In my opinion, the best method for searching an online database for the literature on a particular professional problem is to:

1. Identify the keywords that best represent what you intend to study.
2. For a single online database, use the database's thesaurus to determine the synonyms used to catalog the information in that database for each of your keywords. [Caveat: You must search each online database separately, since each database has a different method of cataloging information and, hence, its own unique thesaurus.]
3. Using the synonyms for each of your keywords, search the database for articles that simultaneously match all of your keywords.

4. Repeat the process as necessary with other databases to identify a researchable dissertation topic.

An example should help to clarify the method.

Step 1

As part of the first step in applying this method, I strongly suggest that you try to encapsulate the focus of your big idea in a tentative dissertation title. This exercise demands a level of attention to detail that is both necessary and helpful. For the sake of illustration, let us use the title of my dissertation (which contains the gist of what I studied in my research) as the starting point:

The Impact of a Transforming Leadership Style on Follower Performance and Satisfaction: A Meta-Analysis

The keywords in this title are (a) transforming leadership, (b) outcomes (e.g., follower performance or satisfaction), and (c) meta-analysis.

In short, my study was about how one particular style of leadership affects workers' behavior, and the research method I used was a quantitative one called meta-analysis.

You will probably not want to restrict your initial literature search by the type of research method, as you will want to identify all of the studies on your potential dissertation topic. This broader search (i.e., one not limited to a particular research method) might provide valuable ideas on how to approach your topic that you would never have thought of and should consider.

With this very important proviso, let us proceed with an examination of the second step in the method using my keywords as a concrete example.

Step 2

In Business Source Premier, a management database, I used the thesaurus to identify the corresponding keyword used in that database's thesaurus for each of the three keywords in my search. The following table shows the results.

Table 9. Results of Using a Database Thesaurus

Original Keyword	Thesaurus Keyword
Transforming leadership	LEADERSHIP
Outcomes	No Match (So I used the original keyword Outcomes)
Meta-analysis	META-analysis

[Note: Each database may have a different keyword in its thesaurus for a given keyword of yours. So, be sure to go through this same conversion with each database you decide to search.]

Step 3

The third step in the method requires that you search simultaneously for articles which match ALL of the thesaurus keywords corresponding to your original keywords. Common sense suggests that a search for any one of the keywords, while it will yield a much larger number of articles, will not be as helpful to you in grounding your big idea as a search which requires that the selected articles match all of your keywords.

For example, a search using the keyword LEADERSHIP yielded approximately 22,000 articles. The first of these was entitled, "Veiling the Obvious: African feminist theory and the hijab in the African novel," which is hardly what I was looking for as a grounding study.

On the contrary, a search using all three keywords (i.e., LEADERSHIP and Outcomes and META-analysis) resulted in 17 articles, all of which were much more on target, and one of which was the article I used to ground my dissertation work (DeGroot, Kiker, and Cross, 2000). [Note: When I was a student I did not know how to use this method. So I had to search and search until I found DeGroot, Kiker, and Cross (2000). If I had known about this powerful method of searching databases at the time, it would certainly have made my task much easier.]

That said, it is important to note that this method is not perfect, and hence does not always work. For example, when I substituted the keyword Performance for Outcomes, I got 36 hits, but they did not include DeGroot, Kiker, and Cross (2000). Similarly, when I substituted Satisfaction for Outcomes, I got 17 hits, but they also did not include DeGroot, Kiker, and Cross (2000).

Step 4

Hence, as the fourth step in the method suggests, like most other aspects of doctoral-level work (which is more art than science), you may need to use the method in a trial-and-error or iterative manner (using related keywords) to find the set of articles that define the body of prior research literature in your field of study.

Despite any inherent shortcomings, this method is a very efficient way to search, and I recommend that you use it to help you search for and find the grounding literature for your dissertation topic.

Appendix B

Developing Hypotheses

Quantitative research involves the statistical analysis of study data to test pre-determined hypotheses based on the research questions. Hence, it is important to know how to create appropriate hypotheses. The following are some suggestions for doing this:

1. There is always a null and an alternative hypothesis for each research question.
2. The null hypothesis always includes the status quo.
3. When there is no strong prior evidence (in the literature), the hypotheses must be non-directional. When there is strong prior evidence, then the hypotheses may be directional.
4. The correct statistical analysis for testing the hypothesis depends on the research design.
5. As a result of the appropriate statistical test, you either reject the null or you do not.
6. Regardless of how significant the results of a hypothesis test are, it does not prove anything.

To illustrate these points, we will use two examples of research questions and their associated hypotheses:

Example A

RQ: *How much of an effect does leadership style have on follower satisfaction?*

H_0: Leadership style has no effect on follower satisfaction.

H_a: Leadership style has an effect on follower satisfaction.

Example B

RQ: *How much more effective is a modern leadership style than a traditional style?*

H_0: A modern leadership style is less than or equal to a traditional style in effectiveness.

H_a: A modern leadership style is more effective than a traditional style.

An inspection of both examples shows that they have the required null and alternative hypothesis structure and that the null hypothesis includes the status quo—there is no relationship in the first case, and the new drug is equal to the best existing one in the second case. The major difference between these two examples is that the first example does not specify the direction of the relationship between leadership style and follower satisfaction. If there is a relationship, it may be positive or negative in the sense a change in style may cause satisfaction to increase (positive) or decrease (negative). Either way, if the difference is statistically significant, we will be justified in rejecting the null hypothesis that there is no relationship between them (i.e., that leadership style does not affect follower satisfaction) in favor of the alternative hypothesis that there is a relationship. In contrast, in the second example, which specifies the directional impact of the independent variable (modern leadership style) on the dependent variable (effectiveness), we will be justified in rejecting the null hypothesis only if the measured difference in effectiveness is positive (more effective) and statistically significant. If it is equal to or less effective or it is not statistically significant, we will not reject the null. Hence, the direction of the difference from the status quo or null is important when the hypotheses are directional.

So how do you decide whether to create non-directional hypotheses (Example A) or directional hypotheses (Example B) for the quantitative research questions in your study? The answer depends on the findings of previous research studies reported in the academic literature of your field. If the number of studies is extensive and the findings indicate a strong relationship, then you would be justified in specifying directional hypotheses. If this is not the case, then you should specify non-directional hypotheses. In either case, you must not base your decision on your personal opinion of the relationship, regardless of how much practical experience you have that relates to the variables in your study.

The decision of what statistical method to use to test your hypotheses depends on the type of research question, and the type and number of variables in your study. For instance, if the measurements for leadership style and follower satisfaction in Example A produced interval or ratio scale data, calculating a simple (Pearson product-moment) correlation coefficient and assessing its statistical significance would be sufficient to test the hypotheses and thereby answer the research question. Alternatively, if the measurement of leadership style resulted in a simple distinction between modern and traditional leadership (which is nominal scale data), then the appropriate test would be a *t*-test of the difference between the means (averages) of two independent groups—the average satisfaction of those people in the sample who have a modern leader versus the average satisfaction of those who have a traditional leader (Example A), or the average effectiveness of those people in the sample who have a modern leader versus the average effectiveness of those who have a traditional leader (Example B).

Regardless of the result of a hypothesis test, you must state your conclusion in relation to the null, not the alternative. For example, saying that you fail to reject the null hypothesis based on the results of the statistical analysis is the appropriate terminology for a test that indicates no significant difference between the null and the alternative. Similarly, stating that you reject the null hypothesis in favor of the alternative is the correct way to state the results of test that shows a statistically significant difference between the null and the alternative.

Finally, even if you find a highly significant difference between the null and alternative hypotheses, it is not appropriate to claim that this *proves* that they are different. Given that every theory is only an approximation and that there is always some level of uncertainty associated with any measurement, it is impossible to prove any theory by means of hypothesis testing (i.e., scientific research). So be sure not to make any such claim in your dissertation.

On a related matter, it is important to note that only true experiments, with carefully controlled conditions, can lead to results that demonstrate a causal relationship between the independent and dependent variable. Hence, you cannot make any cause and effect statements based on the findings of any other form of research, such as existing data analysis or correlational (i.e., survey) research. I mention this because many doctoral students start out wanting to prove something is true, and it often involves what they believe to be a causal relationship between one or more independent variables and a one or more dependent variables. Although we have just scratched the surface on the topic, following the suggestions in this appendix should help you to avoid some of the most common errors associated with specifying and testing research hypotheses.

Appendix C

Selecting a Research Method

The first step in selecting the research method best suited to your particular study is to determine if your research questions are qualitative or quantitative in nature. If the questions in some way ask what, why, or how, they are qualitative. Qualitative research methods—such as case study, grounded theory, phenomenology, ethnography, and action research—provide answers to qualitative research questions. Conversely, if the questions ask something about the relationship or the difference between two or more variables, they are quantitative. Quantitative research methods—such as an experiment, quasi experiment, survey, existing data analysis, and meta-analysis—provide answers to quantitative research questions. While a thorough review of the specific requirements of each method is beyond the scope of this book, there is a simple way for you to determine which one or two might best suit your research objectives.

One useful criterion for deciding which research method to use is its primary focus. Table 10 shows the focus of several commonly used qualitative and quantitative research methods. For a qualitative study, if you are planning to examine a bounded system, such as a classroom or a group, to learn more about it, then you should consider using a case study approach. To learn what factors affect something, like what are the elements of an ideal learning environment or what causes resistance to change, or if you wish to go one step further and infer from these factors a theory that explains what is going on, then grounded theory built from a constant comparative analysis of individual observations, one-on-one interviews, or existing documents related to the lived experiences of the study participants would be your best bet. If you are fascinated by a phenomenon, such as why, how, and to what extent patients abuse nurses, then a an in-depth study of a purposive sample of nurses who have experienced the phenomenon first hand using a phenomenological approach might work best. An ethnographic study would help you to understand the effect of a strong group or organizational culture on the behavior of individuals exposed to that culture. Finally, if you wanted to work side-by-side with a group seeking to effect organizational or social change, then a more involved, participatory approach, like action research, might be ideal. In such as study, you would work with the participants to jointly identify the issues that need changing (the research phase), and then plan and execute a series of change initiatives based on your research findings (the action phase). You would then do more research to determine the results of these changes, and perhaps decide to take further action, thus continuing the action/research cycle.

For a quantitative study, such as an experiment, you would plan to control as many of the variables that might affect the outcome as possible, varying only the treatment received by the participants in the test group. If you were unable to control some of the important variables in your study, then you would have to select a quasi-experimental design and manage the threats to internal and external validity of that design to the greatest extent possible. If an experiment or quasi-experiment was not possible, you might choose to obtain some of the data for your study by asking participants to complete one or more survey instruments designed to elicit their perceptions of important variables in your study, such as the leadership style of each participant's manager in an organizational leadership study.

Table 10. Focus of Various Research Methods

Research Method	**Nature**	**Primary Focus of Method**
Case Study	Qualitative	Analysis of a bounded system
Grounded Theory	Qualitative	Experience-based theory development
Phenomenology	Qualitative	Exploration of a specific phenomenon
Ethnography	Qualitative	Study of a culture
Action Research	Qualitative	Participatory change implementation
Experiment	Quantitative	Controlled test of key variables
Quasi-experiment	Quantitative	Partially controlled test of key variables
Survey	Quantitative	Analysis of self-reported perceptions
Existing Data Analysis	Quantitative	Secondary data analysis
Meta-Analysis	Quantitative	Statistical analysis of primary research

Other quantitative study data might be available from existing sources, such as employee performance ratings, sales figures, test scores, and the like. In some cases, the entire study might focus on the analysis of secondary data, such as census data, available from public or private sources. This type of research, based on existing data analysis, when it is possible, saves you the time of having to collect original (i.e., primary) data for your study. Finally, if you are good at statistics and want to examine all of the existing primary quantitative studies (which includes experiments, quasi-experiments, surveys, and existing data analyses) on a particular (assumed to be) cause and effect relationship between an independent and a dependent variable, then performing a meta-analysis of their findings (in effect, an analysis of the analyses presented in each of the primary research studies in your population of studies) might provide some important new evidence on the strength of that important relationship. [Note: To learn more about one or more of these research methods to evaluate its applicability to your proposed dissertation research, you should read a methodology manual for it, like one of those presented earlier in the selected readings section of the book.]

Appendix D

Developing the Model

Every quantitative study has an underlying model. It may be as simple as the general one below, which expresses the relationship between a single independent variable (X) and a single dependent variable (Y), or it may be much more complicated.

$$Y = f(X)$$

In this formula, f stands for "a function of." Thus, the formula says that Y is a function of X, which means that the value of Y depends on the value of X.

For a study involving the quantification of the relationship between two variables, one independent (X) and one dependent (Y), as measured by simple regression analysis, the specific underlying model takes this form:

$$Y = a + b^*X + \text{Error}$$

Note that the letters *a* and *b* in this model stand for parameters, which are numbers whose value depends on the sample data used to compute them.

If the study focuses on quantifying the relationship between more than one independent variable (X_1, X_2, to X_n) and one dependent variable (Y) based on a multiple regression analysis, the specific underlying model takes this form:

$$Y = b_0 + b_1{}^*X_1 + b_2{}^*X_2 + \ldots + b_n{}^*X_n + \text{Error}$$

It is important to note that for each model used to capture the relationship between the independent and dependent variables in a study, there is a corresponding computational method to determine the values of the model parameters (such as b_0 to b_n in the model above), as well as an associated statistical analysis method to compute the relevant statistics related to the model and its parameters. [Note: Further discussion of models and computational methods, which gets very complicated very quickly, is beyond the scope of this book. For this reason, you will need to work closely with the methodologist on your dissertation committee to determine the underlying model, variables, and computational methods for your particular quantitative study.]

Appendix E

Selecting the Sample

Sampling theory makes it possible to generalize the findings of a quantitative study based on data collected from a sample to the larger (often much larger) population which the sample represents. However, unless the sample is representative of the target population from which you select it, and the target population is representative of the entire population (as depicted in Figure 6), there is no guarantee that the findings will generalize to the population (i.e., have external validity). A simple example will show why.

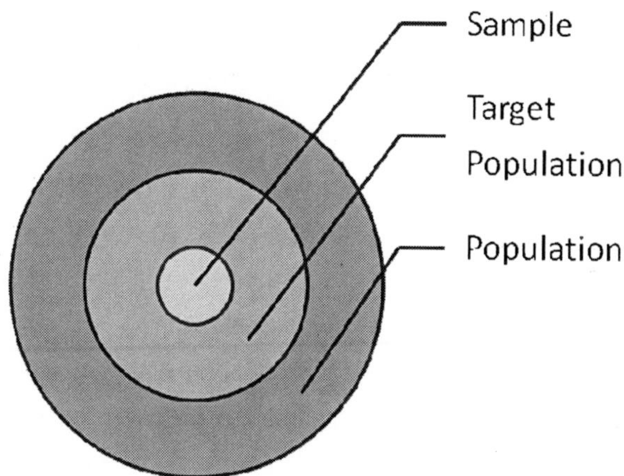

Figure 6. Sample versus Target Population and Population

Imagine that you are trying to estimate the height of the typical student in a particular high school (the population). For this purpose, you decide to measure the first five people who get off the next school bus to arrive in the parking lot (which happens to be returning from an away basketball game). You do this and find that their respective heights (in inches) are 72, 74, 76, 78, and 80, which means the average height of the sample is 76, or 6 feet 4 inches. This hardly seems representative of the height of the typical student in the school. So, what went wrong?

As you have no doubt surmised, the problem is that the sample was not representative of the students in the high school. That is because (a) it was too small, and (b) you did not select it at random from the entire school population. Rather you selected it from a target population, the students on the bus, which was not representative of the entire student body. A bigger sample (preferably greater than 30 per the Central Limit Theorem of statistics) drawn randomly from students in the entire school would have yielded a much better estimate of the height of the average student at the high school. You might have done this by securing a list of all students currently enrolled at the high school (called a sampling frame) and using a random number table to help you draw a systematic sample of about 100 students (a good number for a quantitative study) from the list. [Note: If you are not familiar with the use of systematic sampling for drawing a random sample from a list (i.e., sampling frame) and you want to learn more about it, review a statistics book or other reference on the subject, or perform an Internet search.]

For dissertation research, you must compute a specific minimum sample size for the type of statistical test you will use to test your hypotheses. In addition to the type of statistical test, the sample size will also depend on several standard criteria related to the probability of making a Type I error (falsely rejecting the null hypothesis) or a Type II error (falsely accepting the null hypothesis), as well as the size of the estimated difference between the null value and the alternative value that you are trying to measure. For example, if you planned to use a simple (Pearson product-moment) correlation coefficient to measure the relationship between each independent variable and the dependent variable in your study, you would do an *a priori* (i.e., in advance) power analysis involving (a) a two-tailed *t*-test, (b) the standard or medium effect size (i.e., difference between alternative value and the null value you are trying to measure) for a correlation statistic of .30, (c) the standard significance level of 5%, (d) and the standard power of 80%. The result would be a minimum required sample of 82. To complete the requirements for the generalizability of your findings, you would need to draw/select these 82 participants in your study at random from the target population of your study.

[Note: If you plan to do a quantitative study, refer to your statistics book for a discussion of how to draw a random sample from your target population using simple or systematic sampling, or stratified sampling (if necessary). If you are using an Internet survey to collect your data, refer to your methodology manual for a more complete discussion of random sampling in that context. Finally, consider doing an Internet search for G*Power, a free software package for computing sample size as a function of the factors mentioned above.]

In a qualitative study, your objective is different. You typically need a sample of 10 to 20 participants who know something about the issue or phenomenon you are studying because they have personally experienced it. To ensure that your sample consists of such people, you must select your participants on purpose. This purposive sampling approach is a non-probability sampling process, in contrast to the random/probability sampling process used in a quantitative study. The techniques for identifying such participants have many names (such as purposive, emergent, snowball, and theoretical sampling). Regardless of the name, the basis for all of these qualitative sampling methods is essentially the notion of selecting people who know something about what you are interested in studying because they have experienced it firsthand. [Note: The price you pay for enhancing the validity of your findings by selecting a purposive sample, rather than drawing a sample at random from the population, is that you cannot generalize the findings of your study from the sample to that larger population. However, a well executed qualitative study based on a carefully selected purposive sample can be very credible to those who read it; causing them to see its findings as directly applicable to others in the population beyond the sample chosen for the study. In short, while you cannot make the claim of generalizability for your qualitative findings (as quantitative researchers can), your readers can, in effect, make it for you by acting on your findings.]

Another sample-related issue in qualitative research involves knowing when to stop sampling. In quantitative research, you stop when you have a number of completed, error free data sets/responses equal to your minimal sample size. If you have more, so much the better; but you only need a number equal to the required sample size (which in the example above was 82). In most qualitative research, you stop when your analysis of the next qualitative data set (i.e., interview, observation, or document) does not increase your understanding of the situation. In practice, you may need to complete one or more additional analyses to confirm that you are not learning anything new, but at some point you will know that you have reached the *saturation* point and it is time to stop collecting and analyzing data.

Appendix F

ABCs of APA Style

Conceived in the 1920s to make the process of communication among scholars via the publication of manuscripts easier and more effective, the style guidelines of the American Psychological Association are widely used in universities and in scholarly journals today (American Psychological Association, 2010, p. xiii). APA style is convenient shorthand that fosters universal communication among scholars. Therefore, like it or not, anyone who wants to communicate with other scholars via the journals that require APA (or those students whose universities require them to format their dissertations according to APA guidelines) has to learn at least the basics, or ABCs, of APA style.

ABC analysis, also known as 80-20 analysis, focuses on the few items that make the biggest difference. Doing this maximizes efficiency and effectiveness. For example, the management of a retail store with 1000 items for sale would want to know which of those items had the highest demand so they could manage their inventory to ensure that they always had sufficient quantities of the best sellers in stock to meet customer demand. Whether or not they ran out of stock on the infrequently selling items (i.e., the *trivial many*) would be much less important to them, and, therefore, would receive much less of their time and attention. Typically, a very small percentage of the items (generally 20% or less) account for the highest percentage of sales (generally 80% or more); hence the term 80-20 analysis. The former, known as the *vital few* items, are the ones that the store must identify and manage most carefully.

Many students are new to the nuances of American Psychological Association (APA) style and find the process of using it to format their dissertations somewhat confusing, which is not surprising as learning APA is like learning a foreign language, a necessary but daunting task. To make that task easier, in this section you will find concrete information about how to write correct APA citations easily, both in the body of your dissertation and in your reference lists, for those *vital few* sources of information that constitute the most frequently encountered reference citations. For the *trivial many* sources that constitute the least frequently encountered reference citations, which coincidentally require the most expert guidance to get right, you (like me) have the APA manual to help you with.

Common Reference Sources (The Vital Few)

While there seems to be no end to the variety of sources of scholarly evidence—such as periodicals, books, audiovisual sources, and electronic sources—some arise more frequently in scholarly research than others. If you glance at the reference list of any journal article, you will find that most of the references are for journal articles and books. Since, these constitute the *vital few* which writers must understand and use correctly if they wish to earn recognition as scholars, we will focus on them. However, before we get started, we need to cover a few preliminaries.

Cite Properly, Avoid Plagiarism

It is paramount in scholarly writing to support every assertion you make with a reference to the literature. This both bolsters your argument and ensures that the person whose ideas you are using to make your case receives full credit for them. Failure to cite the work of others (thereby creating the impression that the ideas are yours), whether intentional or not, constitutes plagiarism. Plagiarism is intellectual property theft, and is, of course, completely unacceptable.

Good Things Come in Pairs

To cite a source properly in a paper (or other formal document), a writer must (a) describe it briefly in the text, and (b) provide enough additional information in the list of references so that a reader could find that source in the literature. The in-text citation provides pertinent information required for the identification of the source, and, in effect, points to the full, bibliographic reference citation provided in the reference list, where the reader can find the rest of the relevant information on the source. [Note: You must provide both an in-text citation and a reference citation for each source. Also, you must cite only sources that you have personally read.]

Anatomy of a Book Citation

Several years ago, I wrote and published a book to help new doctoral students accelerate their progress toward the degree. In it, I shared my ideas, as a recent Ph.D. graduate and full-time doctoral faculty member at a leading online university, for achieving this ultimate educational goal as cost-effectively as possible. This book is entitled *Student to Scholar: The Guide for Doctoral Students* (Levasseur, 2006).

Let us imagine that you read my book and decide to use some of the ideas in your writing. In particular, you want to write, based on your own experiences, about the importance of starting to think about your dissertation early in your doctoral program. To that end, you decide to quote a passage from my book before introducing your own critical ideas on the subject based on your experiences as a doctoral student. Hence, you write:

> Traditional thinking says that you should start by studying your field (e.g., management, psychology, education) and then,

> when and only when you are ready, embark on your dissertation work. In practice this leads to a more or less linear process of course work, major papers, and the dissertation. While there is nothing inherently wrong with linear notion, you must not follow it strictly if you want to accelerate your program. (Levasseur, 2006, p. 9)

In this block quote, (Levasseur, 2006, p. 9) is the in-text citation.

This in-text citation identifies who wrote the quoted material and when, as well as the exact page (or pages) from which the quotation came, but it does not identify the nature of the source. That is, it does not tell a reader whether the referenced material comes from a book, a journal article, a dissertation, or some other source. The full reference citation, which you provide in the reference list, completes the picture.

Here is the reference citation for my book:

Levasseur, R. E. (2006). *Student to scholar: The guide for doctoral students.* Annapolis, MD: MindFire Press.

Now the reader knows (by its format) the rest of the story. Namely, that the quoted material comes from a book. Note that the reference citation contains (a) additional information about the author's name (to specify the exact writer or writers, if there are several authors), (b) the full title of the book (with only the first letter of the title and of the subtitle in capital letters—except, of course, for any proper nouns, like America or Australia, which you must also capitalize), and (c) the location and name of the publisher. As you will soon see, the reference citation for a journal article is noticeably different from this basic form for a correct, APA style book reference citation.

Anatomy of a Journal Article Citation

Journal article reference citations constitute the most common type of reference found in scholarly publications, because the number of such articles published in a field on a given topic typically far exceeds the number of books or other sources. For the sake of illustration, let us imagine that you once again want to quote a passage from one of my published works to support a point of view expressed in another one of your papers. However, this time you are paraphrasing a section of a journal article.

> Many social science researchers have examined the impact of processes that induce cooperation in groups versus that of processes that instigate competition or create internal conflict. An aggregate analysis (a meta-analysis) of over 500 such studies by Johnson and Johnson (1989) showed that cooperative processes are far superior to conflict-inducing, competitive processes in terms of group performance and member satisfaction. (Levasseur, 2005, p. 179)

In this block quote, (Levasseur, 2005, p. 179) is the in-text citation.

As with the in-text citation for the book, this in-text citation identifies who wrote the quoted material and when, as well as the exact page from which the quotation came, but does not identify the nature of the source. To complete the picture, here is the reference citation for the journal article:

Levasseur, R. E. (2005). People skills: Change management tools—leading teams. *Interfaces, 35*(2), 179–180. doi:10.1287/inte.1050.0132

Now the reader knows (by its format) that the quoted material comes from a journal article. Note that the reference citation contains (a) additional information about the author's name (for positive identification), (b) the full title of the article, as well as (c) the journal title, volume number, issue number (in parentheses), the beginning and ending pages of the article, and the digital object identifier (doi). The doi number enables searchers of online databases to find the article more easily. [Note: We will have more to say about the doi number later in this appendix.]

Comparison of Book and Article Citations

There are some subtle ways in which APA style requires you to present features of your reference citations which bear further examination. To facilitate this comparison, we need to study the two reference citations again.

Levasseur, R. E. (2006). *Student to scholar: The guide for doctoral students.* Annapolis, Maryland: MindFire Press.

Levasseur, R. E. (2005). People skills: Change management tools—leading teams. *Interfaces, 35*(2), 179–180. doi:10.1287/inte.1050.0132

Note first that the name of the book is in italics. Highlighting with italics draws the reader's attention to the location of the quoted material (i.e., in the 2006 edition of *Student to Scholar*).

Similarly, the title of the journal (i.e., Interfaces) and the volume number (i.e., 35) are in italics. This makes clear to the reader the specific location of the quoted material (i.e., in Volume 35 of Interfaces). [Caveat: Do not italicize the issue or page numbers of the journal article.]

Note very carefully the way in which APA captures the information on each source presented in the respective citations. Namely, the last name of the primary author comes first, followed by the initials (not the full name) of the author's first name (and, in this case, middle name). Pay particular attention to the spacing between those initials (i.e., R. E., not R.E.) and between the initials and the year of publication. The year of publication (i.e., 2006) is in parentheses followed by a period.

The title of the article and the book are subject to the same rules of capitalization. That is, capitalize only the first letter of the first word of the title (and of the subtitle if there is one) as well as any proper nouns, like England or France. In contrast, you must capitalize all of the major words in the journal's title.

The location of the publisher, followed by a colon, a space, and the name of the publisher, come last in a book reference citation. The journal title, volume, issue, page range, and the doi number complete a journal article reference citation. [Caveat: Do not insert a p. or pp. before your page range. It is neither necessary, nor acceptable. Also, note the spacing between required elements of the citation.]

The doi number is a new requirement driven by the move to electronic publishing. It serves as a permanent link to the article, replacing the retrieval information required by earlier editions of the APA manual. You can find the doi number for an article in the article information provided on the landing page of the article in an online data base. Alternatively, you can use the crossref website (http://www.crossref.org/SimpleTextQuery/) to identify the doi number, if one exists. Once you have found it, format the doi as shown in the example above. If you cannot find a doi number, then provide the URL of the home page of the journal that published the article (which you can find by doing an Internet search using the journal name as the keyword). In those rare cases when neither is available (as with classic articles published in journals no longer in print but available as online documents), then provide the URL of the database from which you downloaded the article.

A Sample Reference List

To cement the ideas we have covered so far, let us examine the following list of citations excerpted from the reference list of Barling, Weber, and Kelloway (1996), an excellent article on the effects of transforming leadership:

Barling, J., Fullugar, C., & Kelloway, E. K. (1992). *The union and its members: A psychological approach.* New York, NY: Oxford University Press.

Conger, J. A., & Kanungo, R. N. (1987). Toward a behavioral theory of charismatic leadership in organizational settings. *Academy of Management Review, 12*, 637–647. doi:10.2307/258069

Drucker, P. F. (1995, February). Really inventing government. *Atlantic Monthly, 275*(2), 49–52, 54, 56, 57, 60, 61. Retrieved from http://www.theatlantic.com/

[Note: The first reference citation is for a book and the last two are for articles. Also, note that the order of the citations is alphabetical, based on the last name of the primary author.]

Each citation has a unique feature that makes it different from the very basic form for a book or a journal article shown earlier. Let us analyze some of these unique characteristics.

First, the first two reference citations have multiple authors, which is something that happens frequently in scholarly publication. Note (a) that commas separate the authors' names, (b) that a comma follows the next-to-last name (which is not the practice in general business writing), and (c) that an ampersand (i.e., &) replaces the word *and* before the last author's name. Even when there are only two authors, as in the second reference citation, a comma still separates the names, and an ampersand still precedes the name of the second author.

Second, the third reference citation, for a magazine article, while similar to a journal article citation, does differ in some respects. Note, particularly, that the month of publication (i.e., February) appears with the year of publication in parentheses, even though the issue number also appears in parentheses after the volume number (i.e., *275*(2)). Also, because there is no doi number for the second article, we use the URL of the journal publisher, the Atlantic Monthly, for the Drucker article.

How would you know that you have to put the month of publication in the reference citation for a magazine article? How would you know that you have to separate multiple authors' names with serial commas and an ampersand? How would you know how to cite any of the myriad of sources of information used in scholarly writing? The answer to these questions is simple. The APA manual, or some other APA guide, would provide you with the necessary information to write each citation correctly.

Avoiding Common APA Errors

Many students make the same errors when they first work with APA style. In this section, we will examine some of the most common situations that confuse doctoral students. The goal is to show you how to avoid making these APA mistakes in your work.

Use of and vs. &

When a source has two or more authors, like Smith and Jones, then follow this simple rule: Separate the names by *and* unless the names appear in parentheses. In that case, separate them by an ampersand (&). For example, to introduce a quotation found on the first page of a hypothetical work by Smith and Jones, you might write:

> Smith and Jones (2000) said, "Write like a scholar" (p. 1).

Alternatively (and equally correctly), you might write:

> "Write like a scholar" (Smith & Jones, 2000, p. 1).

Similarly, you might cite the hypothetical work of three authors in either of these ways:

> Tinker, Tailor, and Toddler (2005) said, "A leopard can't change its spots" (p. 10).
>
> "A leopard can't change its spots" (Tinker, Tailor, & Toddler, 2005, p. 10).

Note the use of *and* or *&* as required.

Serial Comma

In business communication, you typically punctuate three or more terms in a series (e.g., X, Y, Z) as follows: X, Y and Z. However, in APA style, you punctuate them as follows: X, Y, and Z. Note the extra comma after the term preceding the word *and.* Thus, Tinker, Tailor, and Toddler is correct; Tinker, Tailor and Toddler is not.

Location of Quotation Marks and Periods

Which is correct, A, B, or C?

A. "Write in the active voice." (English, 2010, p. 1)

B. "Write in the active voice." (English, 2010, p. 1).

C. "Write in the active voice" (English, 2010, p. 1).

If you said C you are paying attention, since we covered this quotation earlier. Think of C as a complete sentence that includes the quote and the in-text citation, and which, therefore, requires a concluding period. What is the difference between A and B? [Hint: It has to do with the periods.]

Note that if your direct quotation is 40 or more words in length, you must present it in block quote form, like this:

> Traditional thinking says that you should start by studying your field (e.g., management, psychology, education) and then, when and only when you are ready, embark on your dissertation work. In practice this leads to a more or less linear process of course work, major papers, and the dissertation. While there is nothing inherently wrong with linear notion, you must not follow it strictly if you want to accelerate your program. (Levasseur, 2006, p. 9)

In the case of a block quote, (a) there are no quotation marks, (b) you indent the entire quotation by one-half inch from the left margin, (c) the in-text citation follows the period in the concluding sentence, and, therefore, (d) there is no period after the in-text citation. [Note: While APA requires the indentation by one-half inch of block quotes and reference citations in APA style documents (such proposals and dissertations), the indentations in this appendix are set at one-quarter inch to match the format of the rest of the book.]

Volume and Issue

Which is correct, A, B, or C?

A. Levasseur, R. E. (2005). People skills: Change management tools—leading teams. *Interfaces*, 35(2), 179–180. doi:10.1287/inte.1050.0132

B. Levasseur, R. E. (2005). People skills: Change management tools—leading teams. *Interfaces*, *35*(2), 179–180. doi:10.1287/inte.1050.0132

C. Levasseur, R. E. (2005). People skills: Change management tools—leading teams. *Interfaces*, *35(2), 179–180.* doi:10.1287/inte.1050.0132

The correct answer is B, but why? [Hint: It has something to do with what you must italicize in a journal article citation. Answer: You must italicize the volume number, but not the issue number or page range.]

Use of p.

When you provide the exact page specification in an in-text citation for a quotation (which is necessary) or a paraphrase (which is recommended) to help the reader find the text in the original source if desired, you must include it as follows:

Conger and Kanungo (1987, p. 640).

Note the space between the abbreviation for page (i.e., p.) and the page number (i.e., 640).

If the citation is from more than one page, then it might look like this:

> Conger and Kanungo (1987, pp. 642–643).

As mentioned previously, in reference citations you must not insert a p. or pp. before your page range. It is neither necessary, nor acceptable. A comparison of the two in-text citations above to the reference citation below illustrates this point:

Conger, J. A., & Kanungo, R. N. (1987). Toward a behavioral theory of charismatic leadership in organizational settings. *Academy of Management Review, 12*, 637–647. doi:10.2307/258069

Indenting Reference Citations

In the reference list, start the first line of each reference citation at the left margin. Indent all subsequent lines in the reference citation by one-half inch. Alternatively, use the paragraph formatting feature of your software to create a half-inch hanging indent to achieve the same spacing and allow you to make changes without having to reformat your references. (The machine will do it for you automatically while preserving the hanging one-half inch indentation). [Note: Because it greatly facilitates providing feedback on APA citation errors, I require that my students use the latter method. I highly recommend that you do too.]

As an example, here is the sample reference list provided earlier:

References

Barling, J., Fullugar, C., & Kelloway, E. K. (1992). *The union and its members: A psychological approach.* New York, NY: Oxford University Press.

Conger, J. A., & Kanungo, R. N. (1987). Toward a behavioral theory of charismatic leadership in organizational settings. *Academy of Management Review, 12,* 637–647. doi:10.2307/258069

Drucker, P. F. (1995, February). Really inventing government. *Atlantic Monthly, 275*(2), 49–52, 54, 56, 57, 60, 61. Retrieved from http://www.theatlantic.com/

[Note: Do not bold the word References, as it is the title of the list of citations that follows, not a heading.]

Capitalizing Titles and Subtitles

Although we covered this already, so many people make this particular mistake that it is worth mentioning again.

Which of these two hypothetical reference citations is correct?

Smith, J., & Jones, M. (2010). The Migration of Similar Birds: An Integrative View. *No Such Journal, 26*(3), 1–4. Retrieved from http://www.nosuchjournal.com/

Smith, J., & Jones, M. (2010). The migration of similar birds: An integrative view. *No Such Journal, 26*(3), 1–4. Retrieved from http://www.nosuchjournal.com/

[Answer: The second one is correct. The title and subtitle of the first citation have many words in capital letters that should be in lower case.]

Avoiding Plagiarism when Citing

Many students inadvertently plagiarize when they are first learning APA style. Three primary ways in which this happens are (a) when students rely too heavily on direct quotations, (b) when they fail to use their own words when paraphrasing, and (c) when they fail to provide an in-text and reference citation for a source they are quoting or paraphrasing. Let's examine each type of error briefly.

Problem A: Too Many Quotes

A rule of thumb about quotations that I encourage my students to follow is to keep the percentage of quoted material in each document to less than 10%. The reason for this is simple. Whereas every assertion that a doctoral student makes must have evidence (in the form of a citation from the literature) to support it, the overall work must primarily represent the student's critical thinking, not that of others.

Stringing together a whole series of quotations connected by the odd comment does not constitute doctoral-level work. On the contrary, students must demonstrate their ability to use higher order critical thinking skills by analyzing (i.e., comparing and contrasting), synthesizing, and evaluating the work of others. Just understanding and being able to explain and apply the ideas of others is not enough in doctoral work. So, how does a doctoral student get off the horns of this dilemma (i.e., having to cite to support critical thinking, but not being able to quote more than 10% of the time)?

Citation of the work of others (to give them credit) is the requirement, not quotation of their work. Citation takes the form of either direct quotation or paraphrasing. Hence, the answer is to paraphrase the work of others most of the time, rather than quoting their work. Use direct quotations only in those few instances when you feel that the author(s)'s own words are necessary to convey the proper message to the reader.

Problem B: Not Using Your Own Words

One of the most common errors of well-meaning students is literally to copy most of the words of another writer for fear of not expressing the ideas properly. While this may look like a compliment to the author, it often results in inadvertent plagiarism. Just changing a few words in the original, even if you provide an in-text and reference citation, is plagiarism.

One good way to avoid this egregious error is to read the original source, put it aside, and then write what you remember in your own words. Then, add the proper citation in APA style. You must do both—rephrase in your own words and provide the proper citation—to avoid plagiarizing the original source.

Here is an example based on one of the earlier quotes:

> Traditional thinking says that you should start by studying your field (e.g., management, psychology, education) and then, when and only when you are ready, embark on your dissertation work. In practice this leads to a more or less linear process of course work, major papers, and the dissertation. While there is nothing inherently wrong with linear notion, you must not follow it strictly if you want to accelerate your program. (Levasseur, 2006, p. 9)

In lieu of this quote (to keep the overall percentage under 10%), imagine that you decide to paraphrase this material. So, after reading and putting it aside, you come up with something like the following: Levasseur (2006) argued that a good way to accelerate a doctoral program is to start thinking about a dissertation topic early in the program (p. 9). This gets at the main point, but in your own words, not the author's.

Problem C: Not Providing Required Citations

By convention, readers of scholarly work consider anything for which you do not provide a citation in your writing to be your idea. So, to avoid plagiarism, review everything you write with an eye toward proper attribution of credit. If you have paraphrased or quoted and provided an in-text and reference citation, then you are fine. However, if you have not, ask yourself this question: Are these my ideas or someone else's? If it is not clear, to be safe provide an in-text citation and a corresponding reference citation in the reference list. In this way, you can attribute others' ideas to them and still express your unique scholarly voice by carefully crafting documents that provide solid evidence in support of your high-level analysis of a given topic.

Conclusion

As stated at the outset, the purpose of this material is to provide you with concrete information that will enable you easily to write correct APA citations, both in your texts and in your reference lists, for those *vital few* sources of information that constitute the majority of reference citations. To that end, we examined the form of the most commonly encountered in-text and reference citations—those for books and journal articles. We also discussed many common situations that lead to errors in applying APA style. Hopefully, you are now better prepared to convey your thoughts in writing using this important language of scholarly communication.

Appendix G

Frequently Asked Questions

In this section, you will find the answers to several questions not otherwise covered in this book that doctoral students frequently ask.

How long does it take to complete a dissertation?

Although this depends on the student and the requirements of the university, it takes at least one to three years for most students to complete a dissertation. The average at my online university is between 1½ to 2 years. At traditional bricks and mortar universities, it may take somewhat longer.

Why does it take so long?

The dissertation is a complex task requiring the application of higher order critical thinking skills to a unique problem by a student who has typically never done a major research project before. Hence, the learning curve is steep. In addition, there are many people who must review and approve the deliverable of each major step in the multi-step dissertation review process. Each of these reviews takes time, as do the revisions often necessitated by the feedback received from these reviews.

What can I do to accelerate the process?

Much of this book is about how to write a high quality dissertation in as short a time as necessary. Among the most important things you can do to achieve this goal are:

- ✓ Select a great chair and committee.
- ✓ Develop a solid IRP as soon as possible after you start on the dissertation journey.
- ✓ Read the APA manual and master its requirements to the greatest degree possible.
- ✓ Write in a precise, straightforward manner that features proper grammar, correct spelling, the active voice, and the proper use of APA style.
- ✓ Quote, paraphrase, and cite sources (both in the text and the reference list) impeccably.
- ✓ Follow your university's dissertation guidelines and writing templates to the best of your ability.
- ✓ Work on your dissertation regularly (every day, if possible). Be persistent and focused.
- ✓ Hone your time management skills.
- ✓ Take advantage of special purpose software packages, and online research management systems (like Zotero and Mendeley), that can facilitate your tasks.
- ✓ Treat all interruptions, no matter how major, as bumps in the road.
- ✓ Develop a solid support system at home, at work, and at school.
- ✓ Check your ego at the door. Be open to the feedback from your committee and university reviewers.
- ✓ Treat all feedback offered to you as constructive input.
- ✓ Carve out time for rest and relaxation so you can stay fresh and avoid burning out.

- ✓ Treat yourself to something special to mark each successful milestone you reach.
- ✓ Visualize yourself crossing the stage at commencement and receiving your academic hood.
- ✓ Do what it takes to maintain your passion for the topic, the journey, graduation, and the promise of what will follow your momentous achievement.

Where can I go for more answers to my questions?

For more answers to questions you may have about dissertation research or the dissertation review process go to http://www.mindfirepress.com/Dissertation_Research.html

How can I contact Dr. L?

I would like to know how you used the information in this book to accelerate your doctoral journey. I would also like to know what, if any, additional information you would like to see in future editions of this book. Finally, I would be happy to answer any question you have that I do not specifically address in the book, this FAQ, or the Dissertation Research website listed on the previous page.

So, please feel free to email me (DrL@mindfirepress.com).

About the Author

Robert E. Levasseur, Ph.D., as a faculty member at several of America's premier online Ph.D. granting universities, teaches doctoral courses and serves on the dissertation committees of students in Leadership and Organizational Change, Public Policy and Administration, Information Systems Management, Engineering, Knowledge Management, Accounting, and Operations Research. His research interests include leadership and organizational change, the application of quantitative methods to decision making, high-performance team development, collaborative meeting management, and organization development/change management. Dr. Levasseur earned undergraduate degrees in physics and electrical engineering from Bowdoin College and MIT, and master's degrees in electrical engineering and management from Northeastern University and the MIT Sloan School of Management, respectively. His Ph.D. is from Walden University.

Dr. Levasseur has taught for Boston University, Franklin University, the International School of Management, Northcentral University, and the University of Maryland University College part-time; and for the University of the Virgin Islands and Walden University full-time. Dr. Levasseur's professional career spanned over three decades, and included positions in leadership, management, and organizational change in Fortune 50 corporations. He is a Registered Organization Development Consultant (RODC) and member of the International Society for Organization Development (ISOD). He is also a member of the Institute for Operations Research and the Management Sciences (INFORMS) and the Systems Dynamics Society. Dr. Levasseur is the author of numerous books and articles. To learn more about his publications, visit Dr. L's website (www.mindfirepress.com).

Books by Robert E. Levasseur

Breakthrough Business Meetings

Professor Edgar Schein of the MIT Sloan School of Management said that *Breakthrough Business Meetings* is "one of the most theoretically sound yet totally practical books on meetings and group management that I have ever read."

Leadership and Change in the 21st Century

Written for the student, scholar, and thoughtful practitioner, *Leadership and Change in the 21st Century* contains theoretical and practical insights that every modern leader needs to know to tackle the important problems of the 21st century.

Practical Statistics

Written in non-mathematical terms for anyone who wants to learn basic statistics for work, school, research, or the sheer enjoyment of gaining new knowledge, *Practical Statistics* focuses on the practical application of statistics to decision making.

Student to Scholar

Student to Scholar is a must if you are currently a doctoral student or expect to be one soon, and you want to get the most out of the time, money, and effort you invest in your doctoral program.

Lightning Source UK Ltd.
Milton Keynes UK
UKOW04f0135190913

217476UK00001B/114/P

9 780978 993030